Library Technology
REPORTS
Expert Guides to Library Systems and Services

Accessibility, Technology, and Librarianship

Heather Moorefield-Lang, Editor

ALA TechSource
alatechsource.org

American Library Association

Library Technology REPORTS

ALA TechSource purchases fund advocacy, awareness, and accreditation programs for library professionals worldwide.

Volume 54, Number 4

Accessibility, Technology, and Librarianship

ISBN: 978-0-8389-1613-1

American Library Association

50 East Huron St.
Chicago, IL 60611-2795 USA
alatechsource.org
800-545-2433, ext. 4299
312-944-6780
312-280-5275 (fax)

Advertising Representative

Samantha Imburgia
simburgia@ala.org
312-280-3244

Editor

Samantha Imburgia
simburgia@ala.org
312-280-3244

Copy Editor

Judith Lauber

Production

Tim Clifford

Editorial Assistant

Colton Ursiny

Cover Design

Alejandra Diaz

Library Technology Reports (ISSN 0024-2586) is published eight times a year (January, March, April, June, July, September, October, and December) by American Library Association, 50 E. Huron St., Chicago, IL 60611. It is managed by ALA TechSource, a unit of the publishing department of ALA. Periodical postage paid at Chicago, Illinois, and at additional mailing offices. POSTMASTER: Send address changes to Library Technology Reports, 50 E. Huron St., Chicago, IL 60611.

ALA TechSource
alatechsource.org

About the Editor

Heather Moorefield-Lang is an associate professor at the University of South Carolina in the School of Library and Information Science. Her research is focused on emerging technologies and their use in education and libraries. Her current research focuses on makerspaces and their integrated technologies in libraries of all types and levels.

Abstract

This issue of *Library Technology Reports* (vol. 54, no. 4), "Accessibility, Technology, and Librarianship," edited by Heather Moorefield-Lang, looks into the wide definition of accessibility for library patrons, both face-to-face and online, within the area of instruction. This topic is discussed in some depth in schools of library science as well as in faculty development and instructional design. This report will encourage readers to think more critically about the technologies that faculty and staff use to address the needs of all patrons served. This report will also aid in identifying and using new methods for addressing the needs of all patrons through a wide range of modalities (closed-captioning, transcription, sign language, video, text to speech, image to text, etc.).

Subscriptions

alatechsource.org/subscribe

Contents

Contents, continued

Chapter 1

Introduction

Heather Moorefield-Lang

It all started with a conversation about YouTube channels and closed-captioning. I have two separate YouTube channels with two separate audiences in mind. The first is titled Tech 15. I created this channel in 2014 with the intention of making short two-to-five-minute videos focusing on different technology tools and sites as well as how each could be integrated into classroom and library instruction. My second YouTube channel is newer and called Research Xpress. I created it to help middle school, high school, and early college students with step-by-step research skills from finding research and information to presenting and citing research. It is a clearinghouse of videos to aid students and the educators and librarians who work with them. All of the videos housed on each channel are closed-captioned for full access and licensed for Creative Commons sharing. The idea behind both channels is to look with an eye toward Universal Design for Learning and accessibility for all students.

Tech 15
https://www.youtube.com/TechFifteen

Research Xpress
http://www.youtube.com/ResearchXpress

Universal Design for Learning (UDL) focuses on the effort to expand and improve teaching and learning for all students based on how they learn.[1] When we make learning available to our students and library patrons through technology, it is imperative that this learning be accessible to all. What this means is that a person who is differently abled can gain the same information, have the same interactions, and be afforded the same instruction as someone who is not identified as differently abled, preferably with ease of use.[2] Accommodations such as closed-captioning, documents for screen readers, and voice-to-text software are some of the ways to make learning more accessible and universal.

In this issue of *Library Technology Reports*, we will look at accessibility, technology, and librarianship across a wide spectrum. Ida Mae Craddock will discuss using virtual reality and Google Expeditions with second language learners. Helen Turner and Patrick Lee Lucas will delve into universal design and providing equitable access to students in the University of Kentucky's College of Design. George Shaw will investigate instruction and access for students taking an online computer programming course. Making library materials accessible to readers through PDF scanning will be the focus of Robert Browder's contribution to this report. Stacy Brown will discuss the impact of littleBits with students at the K–12 level in libraries. Quality Matters accessibility measures, online instruction, library partnerships, and professional development will be the foci of Aisha S. Haynes's discussion. Stacy Hammer will complete our report with a look into the differentiation of instruction in libraries and how technology can be used with our students in the K–12 setting.

There is something for everyone in this report. Authors are from K–12 and academic libraries. They write from schools of library science and other disciplines. The focus remains the same—accessibility for our students and patrons, and an emphasis on the library or on partnerships that include the library.

Audience

I envision the readers of this issue of *Library Technology Reports* to be librarians, classroom teachers, preservice librarians, and professors of library science. In actuality, this report is for anyone looking to find ideas and concepts in the area of accessibility and universal design with technology in learning and instruction. Though we focus on library settings and partnerships, the case studies and ideas shared in this report can easily cross disciplines. We have authors from around the United States represented in this report, but we hope to address the needs of international readers as well. Every chapter written for this report had a specific audience in mind because the authors worked with a certain population. This report was written for the express purpose of generating and sharing ideas as well as to inspire readers to think about learning and methods for making online instruction accessible to all learners and library patrons.

Notes

1. "About Universal Design for Learning," CAST, accessed March 7, 2018, www.cast.org/our-work/about-udl.html.
2. Sheryl Burgstahler, "ADA Compliance for Online Course Design," *Educause Review*, January 30, 2017, https://er.educause.edu/articles/2017/1/ada-compliance-for-online-course-design.

Chapter 2

Immersive Virtual Reality, Google Expeditions, and English Language Learning

Ida Mae Craddock*

A "genius hour" or "20 percent time" is a concept that has been popularized by many major tech giants, including Google, Apple, and 3M. It is a paradigm in which engineers at the company use 20 percent of their workweek pursuing a pet project—something they are passionate or curious about. This concept, now extensively used in educational environments, has proven so effective that it has led to a number of Google products, including Gmail and Google Expeditions.[1]

Google Expeditions was created by Google engineers David Cox and Damien Henry during their 20 percent time.[2] They presented their concept, named Google Cardboard, for the first time at the 2014 Google I/O Developers conference.[3] By 2015, Google had released a kit that included a tablet for teachers, devices for student use, and Cardboard viewers in class sets. According to CNET, it was the first virtual reality (VR) system directly targeted at kids.[4] This focus on children and the classroom experience from the initial development forward has created an experience very different from immersive technologies created for gaming.

While gaming and social networking have driven much of VR content, Google Expeditions (née Cardboard) was born during the 20 percent time of engineers at the Google Cultural Institute and, therefore, has a very different heritage. Education is figuratively in its DNA. While content was initially populated with Google Cultural Institute's museum content, Google Expeditions has quickly added content through partnerships with important institutions including the Smithsonian, the Wildlife Conservation Trust, and the Royal Collection Trust.[5] This has helped keep the quality of the content high.

Nicole Lee's article "Google Makes Its Case for VR by Reinventing the Field Trip" notes that this makes field trips accessible for all students.[6] What is unsaid is that it provides a stepping stool for the students who have the least access to print text in English, travel, and technology—our English language learners (ELLs). ELL students disproportionately benefit from an extremely visual experience that is enhanced by audio narration. Google Expeditions opens up concepts to these students in particular by virtue of its presentation, content, and affordability.

Immersive Virtual Reality in the Classroom

The first time I did an Expedition with a class, I worked with a small group exploring organelles in cell biology. The Expedition was one of four stations in a standard biology class. All the students had to do at the station was experience, watch, and listen. In the first two blocks of the day, there were lots of oohs and aahs. It was fun. It was easy to keep their attention or direct it to points of interest.

There is some value to the "wow" factor in education. Content that engages the learner in a common

* A fifteen-year veteran of Albemarle County (Virginia) Public Schools, **Ida Mae Craddock**, MEd, is the librarian at Burley Middle School. The focus of her research is maker education and the role of school libraries in the community. Her program has been profiled by *School Library Journal*, *Library Media Connection*, NPR, and Edutopia. She has a precocious daughter, an understanding husband, and a lazy dog named Peacha.

experience both creates community and provides a framework and context for the content to be remembered. Engagement in learning, as in Carnini, Kuh, and Klein's 2006 study, correlates to traditional learning outcomes, with students of the least ability benefitting the most.[7] As a classroom teacher of many years, I feel that there is ample anecdotal and commonsense evidence about the links between engagement in learning and outcomes. It is difficult to help kids learn when they do not care. Disinterest is the death knell of any lesson. However, engaging technology will draw student attention to content.

Immersive VR visually blocks out distractions. Not only does it engage students with interesting content, but it also removes anything else competing for visual attention. When we speak about accessibility of content for our students who suffer from attention deficit disorder, anxiety disorders, or impulsivity, a device of this nature literally eliminates distractions. Accessibility takes on many forms; addressing language barriers is one of them. For our ELLs, it helps them concentrate on the content of the visual scene without the stress of decoding written language.

In VR, the value is in perspective. Understanding perspective by (virtually) standing in the shoes of history is a powerful experience. It helps students to think critically about the history that is being taught. While it may be easy to see the pyramids at Giza in the millions of available photographs, immersive VR helps students to stand at the foot of Khufu's pyramid and see the scale of blocks and the distance from water. It may help them understand the engineering involved in the architecture. Measurements and maps say only so much. Standing on the battlefield, on the floor of the Roman Senate, or beneath the glass pyramid at the Louvre helps students understand how events fit together in their context. Rather than presenting stories of lands far away, immersive VR helps history to be that much more real—less about heroes and villains and more about circumstance and humanity.

Unique to immersive VR, the sensation of standing in a scene and being able to turn to see distance, proximity, and perspective helps students think critically about events in history.

Immersive VR and ELL Students

Engaging technology will draw student attention to content. That is exactly what I saw in the first two blocks of that of biology class: student attention focused on organelles.

However, in the last block of the day, I had a group of students who speak English as a second or other language. For them, not only is learning vocabulary words like *mitochondria, endoplasmic reticulum,* and *ribosomes* difficult, but the language barrier makes these terms additionally opaque because the surrounding vocabulary can be an obstacle as well. Words like *powerhouse, highway,* or *control center* pull the content even further out of sight. Not only do the students not understand the actual vocabulary, they also do not understand the metaphors commonly used to explain that vocabulary.

Imagine a scenario in which you not only do not understand that there are tiny things inside cells, you also do not understand the word *cell* or any of the other words your teacher is using while pointing to a squishy-looking graphic on a PowerPoint slide. While ELLs vary in language attainment, the more visual context and clarity the teacher can provide to surround the concept increases the likelihood of comprehension.

By putting students visually inside the cell and by moving from far away to close up in a guided way, language is removed as the necessary component to understanding the concept. As students move through the Expedition with guidance from the teacher, they better understand both the idea of a cell and the idea that there are tiny parts to it that have various functions.

Immersive VR is a visual experience. According to Gersten and Baker's study of effective instructional practices with ELLs, "during English-language content instruction, effective teachers intentionally vary the cognitive and language demands."[8] When the cognitive load is high, as it would be when exploring organelles, language demands should be low. By including immersive VR, the teacher would be keeping the language demands low while increasing the cognitive load. The experience of exploring cells and organelles is a high cognitive load, not only due to the vocabulary, but also due to the concept that tiny invisible working organs control living things. Balancing the demands on student thinking may help with concept attainment, but immersive VR also allows for additionally helpful instructional strategies that are effective for ELLs.

In addition to varying the cognitive and language loads, using inquiry to move through a virtual experience increases science knowledge as well as facility in English language.[9] Posing questions—both the leveled questions offered by Google Expeditions and those offered naturally by the teacher—coupled with the ability to explore in 3-D, makes for a uniquely effective lesson for ELLs.

Why the Library

There is a reason why technologies like immersive VR often find their foothold in schools through the library. First, librarians are both master teachers and subject area generalists who often carry multiple endorsements. Second, one of the foundational concepts of libraries is open access. Technologies that begin in the library are accessible to all teachers and all students.

MLS is not always "master of library science." Sometimes it is "master of looking up stuff." It is one of the tenets of our profession that we can find information faster and better than anyone else in our school building. That includes finding, reading, and applying instructional manuals.

Immersive VR is an addition to our technology offerings. The technology first showed up as a Google Daydream. The Google Daydream is a single-user headset. Students immediately used it for wandering the world using Google Street View, exploring the Dalí Theatre-Museum in Spain, and swimming in the Galapagos using Google Expeditions. The library was the perfect location for students to use VR because it was single user and because it had such varied uses across disciplines.

Librarians teach across all subject areas. In a single week, even those of us on a flexible schedule may teach geometry, biology, language arts, and American history classes. From this position, we are able to demonstrate to teachers best practices in technology integration. One of the AASL's Common Beliefs is, "Qualified school librarians have been educated and certified to perform interlinked, interdisciplinary, and cross-cutting roles as instructional leaders, program administrators, educators, collaborative partners, and information specialists."[10] This cross-cutting role lets us demonstrate to our school communities how immersive VR can be used in whole-class, small-group, and individual instruction. Because librarians are master teachers who coteach, demonstrate, co-plan, and introduce new resources across disciplines, the library is a key component in introducing not just VR, but all kinds of new technologies that should begin their instructional tenures here.

Due to the nature of the library as the heart of a school, it is the one place all students can come to explore ideas and wander through information to create something new. After our experience with immersive VR exploring organelles in biology class, one of the amazing side effects of engagement in learning was joy in learning. All of a sudden, the library was the place to be for ELL students.

Providing access to ideas and information should transcend language. Many of us carry collections in a variety of languages; why would we not use technology in a similar way? Immersive VR allows student access to ideas and information while reducing the cognitive load that ELL students constantly carry. I do not need to wonder why the library in general and immersive VR in particular are popular. Both provide a common experience around common vocabulary without a heavy second language component. It is fun. It makes learning that is fun.

Therefore, the last block of that biology day was a revelation for me. Immersive VR is a technology that can and does transcend a language barrier to both deliver content and enable concept acquisition. Further, it encourages engagement for students in learning and in the library culture. When the library is open to new ideas, new patrons, and new technologies, it is 20 percent time all the time—no matter the subject, no matter the language, no matter which teenage genius is in front of me.

Notes

1. Clint Boulton, "Top 20 Percent Projects at Google," *eWeek*, January 25, 2018, www.eweek.com/networking/top-20-percent-projects-at-google.
2. Nick Statt, "Facebook Has Oculus, Google Has Cardboard," CNET, June 25, 2014, https://www.cnet.com/news/facebook-has-oculus-google-has-cardboard/.
3. Jordan Novet, "Google Announces Cardboard Expeditions to Let Teachers Take Classes on Field Trips," VentureBeat, May 28, 2015, https://venturebeat.com/2015/05/28/google-announces-cardboard-expeditions-to-let-teachers-take-classes-on-field-trips/.
4. Xiomara Blanco, "Google Expedition App Offers VR Field Trips for All," CNET, June 27, 2016, www.cnet.com/news/google-expedition-app-brings-vr-field-trips-for-all/.
5. Lucas Matney, "Google Opens Expeditions VR Education App to the Public," TechCrunch, July 19, 2017, https://techcrunch.com/2017/07/19/google-opens-expeditions-vr-education-app-to-the-public/.
6. Nicole Lee, "Google Makes Its Case for VR by Reinventing the Field Trip," Engadget, AOL, June 4, 2015, https://www.engadget.com/2015/06/04/google-cardboard-vr-education/.
7. Robert M. Carnini, George D. Kuh, and Stephen P. Klein, "Student Engagement and Student Learning: Testing the Linkages," *Research in Higher Education* 47, no. 1 (2006): 1–32.
8. Russell Gersten and Scott Baker, "What We Know about Effective Instructional Practices for English-Language Learners," *Exceptional Children* 66, no. 4 (2000): 465.
9. Elaine Hampton and Rosaisela Rodriguez, "Inquiry Science in Bilingual Classrooms," *Bilingual Research Journal* 25, no. 4 (2001): 417–34.
10. American Association of School Librarians, "Common Beliefs," accessed March 7, 2018, http://standards.aasl.org/beliefs/.

Chapter 3

Curating Technology for Learning

A Faculty View

Helen Turner and Patrick Lee Lucas*

As design faculty, we recognize a wide range of abilities and approaches in learners, and we advocate for creativity, a messy process, and often open-ended opportunities for young designers. Rather than assuming that all students sit as homogenous empty vessels awaiting transfer of knowledge from a sage on the stage, we adopted more active and experiential approaches to teaching and learning as guides on the side.[1] Whether in studio or a more traditional classroom setting, as design faculty we provided ways for students, majors and nonmajors, to see and utilize high-quality images, drawings, diagrams, and text. In uncovering suitable resources to promote quality learning, we regularly deployed video content, virtual experiences, maps, and field experiences along with other geographical data and tools in their work (figure 2.1). Unfortunately, no single source exists for such a wide array of materials. As a result, we often found ourselves navigating the spectrum of materials available on the web and through our own institution's library system, hoping to find, curate, and share exemplary design practices and resulting products. These acts represented some of our biggest challenges as educators teaching in a primarily visual and experiential field.

In this chapter, we unveil approaches to providing equitable access to quality resources through technology from our perspective as faculty members working with and recognizing librarians as partners and willing participants in the academic enterprise. In writing of our successes and challenges in light of the burgeoning wealth of online materials, we share our insights in this essay as committed educators to address the needs of so-called digital natives and the special challenges they bring to the processes of learning. In doing so, we organize our observations and reflections around a design framework with a series of best practices adaptable to almost any field of study.

Approach

We believe that others can learn from design because, frankly, design is everywhere. It is embedded in many processes, spaces, educational systems, technologies, and more. As in other disciplines, professional interior designers have the potential to offer services for research, space planning, and materials selection and strategies for working and doing as well as branding, requiring all types of thinkers and doers. Project-based

* With a master of science degree from the University of Cincinnati and a bachelor of science from Ohio University, **Helen Turner** is also NCIDQ-certified and a LEED-accredited professional with over four years of professional design experience. She is currently an assistant professor with the School of Interiors at the University of Kentucky College of Design, and her interest in sustainability, materials, theory, and digital pathways provides a unique framework for conducting research, pedagogy, and service as a means of expressing the ways in which design adds value to environmental experiences.

Patrick Lee Lucas is the director of the School of Interiors at the University of Kentucky College of Design. An award-winning teacher, Lucas leads seminars, teaches lecture courses, and facilitates studio interactions by engaging in community conversations and encouraging students to think about the place of design in the world. He has led several Education Abroad experiences for students connected to his research agenda about design and community. He serves as the coordinator for international activities in the College of Design.

Figure 2.1
Students visit an Indianapolis Museum of Art installation that artistically questions the efficacy of books as a sole source for knowledge acquisition. Image credit: Turner and Lucas.

studio instruction represents the backbone of interior design education, supplemented by a variety of lecture and skills courses. Aligning with practice, academic programs must draw from creative, open-ended processes alongside technological and measured approaches to understanding human beings. Interior design requires attention to aesthetic qualities in addition to meeting functional conditions that enhance the health, safety, and welfare of humans. In these ways, our work applies to many areas of study.

However, as is the case with all college students and diverse majors, future interior designers come to the university with a wide range of abilities and experiences, as well as with specific approaches and preferences in learning. In response, our faculty brings eighty-plus years of education to the classroom and, with this concentration of knowledge and experience, our program offers students a wide array of teaching philosophies and methods of implementation. Just as design thinking has become an integral strategy for thinking and doing for many outside of design,[2] we hope that our approach to resourcing and curating technology for learning has broad applicability. In these ways, too, our work in curating technology has broad appeal.

As we think about our faculty responsibilities, we recognize a shift in educational practice associated with the technology-infused world of the twenty-first century. The earphones, mobile devices, eyes glued to screens, and moving thumbs visible when walking on a college campus or in the classroom signify the undeniable amount of time students spend plugged in. While a majority of their time may be spent on social networking sites, our faculty believed it possible to engage student interest in the digital world by harnessing a variety of both physical and digital sources to help students better understand how design influences the built environment. Though some educators may avoid technology in their courses, a wealth of virtual platforms, information, and experiences exist that enable modification of the traditional delivery of information to one that embraces technology as a vehicle for learning. This active means of delivery and feedback attracts and informs students of various majors and learning styles and has the potential to make course information relevant by incorporating student enthusiasm for technology. Imagine two scenarios: sitting in an auditorium and listening to an instructor talk about the ancient Roman Colosseum while looking at projected images, or taking a self-directed virtual tour of the historic site with the ability to explore and interact. Which has the greatest potential to impart knowledge and create a meaningful learning experience of the Colosseum?

As designers, we often talk about the seven tenets of universal design: equitable use, flexibility in use, simple and intuitive use, perceptible information, tolerance for error, low physical effort, and size and space for approach and use. These design principles have, in turn, been leveraged to develop Universal Design for Learning principles: multiple means of representation, multiple means of action and expression, and multiple means of engagement.[3] Both sets of design principles emphasize the importance of impactful access to resources. Whether a student is engaged online through computer, tablet, or phone, faculty should take into account students' varying abilities to access and use quality websites, texts, data sets, images, drawings, and videos for coursework and assignments. This includes the option for lecture content, for example, delivered in video or written transcript form or for design ideas to be presented as texts or graphic images, perhaps using a tool like Pinterest as a platform for sharing information.

Moreover, students should be encouraged to produce deliverables in a wide range of modes to enhance learning. Educators must collaborate with librarians and other university partners to ensure these foundational notions apply not only to physical space, but also to the digital world of curriculum development and support.

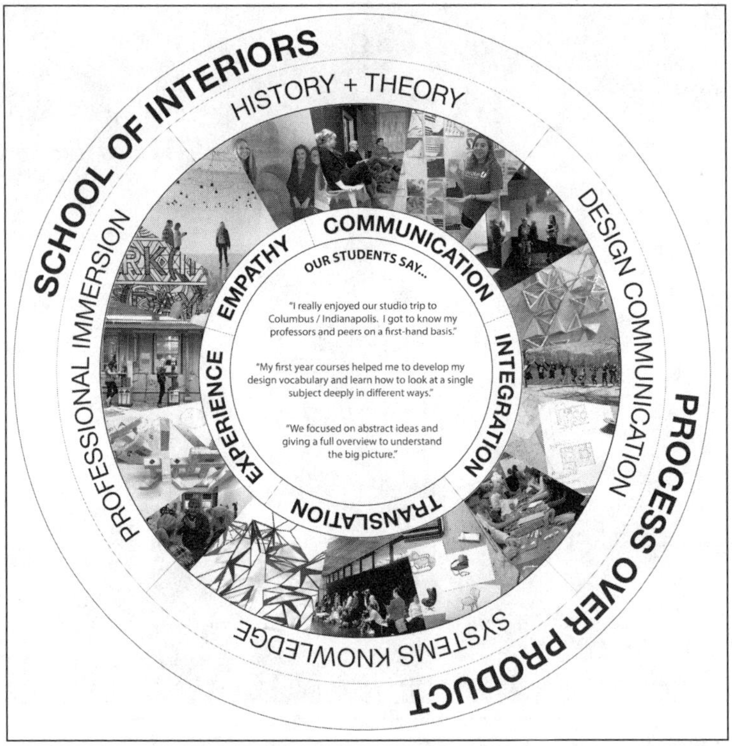

Figure 2.2
Underlying these topical areas for study and using a variety of hand and digital skills, students engage visual representation alongside spoken and written communication to gain information literacy. Image credit: Turner and Lucas.

Recognizing the potential of these strategies to notably impact student learning and faculty teaching, our school strategically forged relationships with librarians and the library system, our professional advisory board, a number of student learners, and educational consultants in our Center for the Enhancement of Learning and Teaching. Doing so reminds us that working as a team provides opportunity for more collective impact than we could ever hope to accomplish on our own. As a group, we designed approaches for a single class, a pair of sequenced courses, and a program-wide platform of resources available to students and faculty, all in support of more meaningful teaching and learning. As a result of these efforts, by the completion of our undergraduate program, young designers have accumulated a breadth of knowledge across an array subject areas: history of the profession, environmental theories on human behavior in space, technical aspects of how buildings are constructed and function, physical materials that build and finish a space, the importance of light and color in experience of space, and business processes of the designer as a professional and communicator of ideas (figures 2.2 and 2.3).

Amid building individual and sometimes overlapping resources accessible to students only during a course through our course management system, our faculty quickly recognized a need for developing an interior design–specific knowledge database through an online portal, known as the Design Drive (figure 2.4). Through this platform, our faculty regularly deploy digital means to deliver lectures, demonstrations, readings, experiences, and guest lectures, thus creating and inculcating hybrid instruction as a pedagogical paradigm shift. The Design Drive has also fostered moments of connection by bringing content into dialog among faculty and students across the program. For instance, one professor might find and share a video about concrete, which illustrates how it is made and how it can be used in building projects. The history course might then use this video to introduce students to the material, but also to indicate how the material has changed since the ancient Roman era, when it was originally created. Then, the interior construction systems course could reference this video to discuss the structural capacity of concrete. Similarly, the interior finish materials course may have students watch the video as a way of expressing the properties and characteristics of concrete as it relates to human interaction, as in a countertop. Finally, a student in a project-based studio course could review the video when specifying and implementing concrete as a design component.

Figure 2.3
To balance the digital content, our school also committed to experiential and active learning, beyond traditional modes of delivery and deliverables, such as field trips, campus building visits, and other forms of engagement. Image credit: Turner and Lucas.

practice with a need to successfully *apply* lessons from the classroom and studio, not just memorize examples for an exam. So our strategy is simple: place some material online in order to free time in the classroom and studio for experiences that allow students to encounter design in the everyday environment with people who live, work, play, and worship in that world alongside peer learners and faculty as guides in the process. Basic understanding comes from online instruction; breadth and depth come from profound, active, and collective experience in the field, sending students to the upper end of Bloom's *Taxonomy of Educational Objectives* and the higher levels in Maslow's Hierarchy of Needs.[4] This approach also permits students to learn more at a self-regulated pace and in an environment suitable to their own learning preferences.

This pedagogical approach has revealed impacts at the course, sequence, and program levels. For instance, in the design introduction course, nonmajors creatively explored emerging ideas about design by examining an object, space, building, or place and its social, historical, and cultural contexts, using a blog as a regular tool to curate their work over the entirety of the experience. Notably, the use of blogs in other courses serves as a method for collecting and curating individual work resulting in unintended consequences where students can use that online catalog to prepare materials for a course in the third year of the program focused on portfolio and personal brand development. Further, utilization of online tools and content in the systems courses has enabled our faculty and students to garner time and space to engage topics directly with local materials, furnishings, and lighting sales representatives and in showrooms. By learning background information online, then seeing materials, furnishings, and lighting firsthand, students experience the tactile qualities of the wide variety and rapidly changing realm of design. Using information learned online alongside experiences in showrooms and sites, they seek materials, furnishings, and installation techniques, then share those to the back to the Design Drive for other students, who then have access to the latest materials in this mercurial world.

Taking advantage of the Design Drive and online content, our faculty have connected students with professionals in a series of five scaffolded interiors profession courses spread across their four undergraduate years. In the first of these courses, students learn about the place of interior design within the varying disciplines of design (architecture, product design, industrial design, urban design). In the second course,

Ultimately these multimodal and hybrid approaches to teaching and learning resulted in making lessons from the classroom relevant to twenty-first-century students in our school and to aspiring young designers as they make their way into professional practice. In the end, we believe our faculty and initiatives have reversed the usual polemic of one-way instruction—handing down of the lore of the discipline from master to apprentice in the studio and classroom—replacing it with a more earthy, nuanced, and immersive experience and introducing a variety of ways to analyze and communicate about design in the past, present, and future. Our students now receive a radically different system for education efforts, which have been recognized by other educators and, more importantly, students in the program. In 2017, the faculty received a national award from the International Interior Design Educators Council (IDEC) for revision of the history and theory course sequence, while one student from the class of 2019 indicated that learning in this hybrid manner supported by online content helps to "form the next generation of design students into impactful leaders who are curious and desire to grow while also finding ways to give back, through design, to our communities."

Impacts

As participants in a professional degree program accredited by the Council for Interior Design Accreditation (CIDA), the majority of our graduates enter students explore pathways they can pursue with an interior design degree. The third course provides space for students to develop their individual brands through a portfolio and website. The fourth class takes students into the field for a shadowing experience. And, finally, in the last course, students learn about business practices and approaches that help them make an easy transition to the world of work. Development of specific online content has allowed more flexibility in taking these courses, for example, while abroad and thus meeting the goal of the program for students to have international experience.

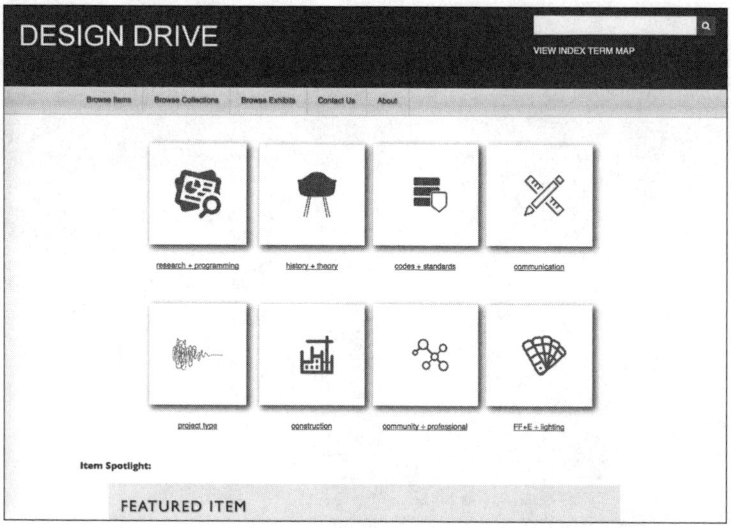

Figure 2.4
As a single-source digital database, the Design Drive serves as the location for wide-ranging materials associated with both the technical and theoretical aspects of interior design necessary for instruction as our school envisioned. Image credit: Turner and Lucas.

Within the history and theory sequence, unit summaries and case studies provided important moments of synthesis, the former about big ideas in units, the latter about the ideas applied to a specific building or design idea in time and space. For these assignments, students pulled ideas from online content, experiences, and their own lives to demonstrate how lessons of history and theory impact the everyday world. As a summative moment for each course in the two-semester sequence, students created a movie. In the first semester, the movie assignment focused on demonstrating proficiency of reading, observing, and recording the built environment. In the second, students examined their own developing approaches to storytelling by reflecting on issues covered in class. Two teaching assistants now lead the teaching in this course under the supervision of a single faculty member, which has allowed undergraduates to have content from the faculty experts who created the content, but has freed these experts to develop other materials and to bring the lessons from the digital realm to other courses in our school.

Above all, students used digital content and the Design Drive to support their active studio practice. They regularly accessed and utilized information gathered on design process, communication techniques, codes, materials, systems, and lighting, initially introduced in other courses. From a studio perspective, students revisited the collected and curated materials as tutorials to help bolster skills and as reminders of approaches, thus saving time and energy of faculty, who would otherwise have to repeat content or instruction that students had undertaken previously. As an extension, the move toward a hybrid digital approach across our curriculum has resulted in students having access to a wider range of materials at a lower cost. Though significant time and resources have been invested in the digital approach to date, the returns are just now being measured. Particularly in a design program where students invest substantially in model making, fabrication, and drawing supplies, the last thing they need to purchase is a textbook that they will use for one class and sell back to the bookstore for less money. We hope the advice in the following section will help others align cost savings with deeper educational opportunities for students, no matter their major.

Best Practices

As design educators, we associate movements and strategies with principles and practices. Thus, the advice presented in this section engages the language of design as a series of best practices determined through reflection on our work over the last three years. As we imagine our initial forays into curating technology for learning in design, we are reminded of the work of mid-twentieth-century design luminaries Charles and Ray Eames, who would advise anyone to remember that design connects at all scales and, as a result, designers should think about both micro- and macroapplications. Similarly, in digital technology, it is helpful to *think both big and small about how technology can be woven with other modes of instruction* in a studio, classroom, and community setting. In addition, in terms of access, the technology should connect to instructional efforts for individual courses as well as contribute to the development of a systems-wide application for all courses in the curriculum. The Eameses would also admit that they do not know everything, but instead bring content and process to help them think holistically. Thus, our admonition is to think like a librarian and, when possible, include librarians in conversations about access, finding quality information, and helping humans understand opportunities for connection.

Working from the perspective of a human-centered process, our faculty initiated a wide range of online content, but also continued to acknowledge the value of in-person lectures and interactions as impactful and necessary for some student learning. Hence, the faculty advocated for all courses to rely on a spectrum of digital opportunities balanced with interpersonal experiences. Our team thus relies on the strengths of individuals or a group of collaborators for generating new and innovative ways of working. Borrowing on an age-old design philosophy, wherein *the whole is greater than the sum of its parts,* these partnerships also catalyzed new modes of thinking and delivery, which eventually trickled down to include student input—from upper-level students as teaching assistants, and eventually primary instructors of some courses, to empowerment of students as generators and contributors of knowledge.

Good designers follow the advice to *measure twice and cut once* to avoid mistakes by thoughtfully considering and accurately proceeding in incremental steps. Given the wide variety of technology and resources available, care should be taken to understand technology before using it and for thinking through how it works before curating into use. Structuring the information within a digital resource like the Design Drive has reminded us that the structure of the resource is also just as important as the content. We also help ourselves think like students by measuring twice through the testing and checking of resources and their access before releasing them. A final lesson of measuring twice reminds us to consider different users and approaches modeled after universal design principles of equitable use, flexibility, intuitive use, and adaptability.

We often tell our students to *work smarter, not harder,* and we believe the Design Drive or other online portals of information create space for shared work and resources, making it easier and more seamless for students and faculty to share in learning. Because faculty guide students and serve as curators and generators of knowledge, they ask that students gain control of their own learning. Faculty and librarians then have the opportunity to serve as facilitators and help guide students to appropriate processes and logical sequences to both access and utilize information in the digital sphere. We assert that this sustainable way of working helps all learners contribute to their own education, thus deepening and enriching collective experience, which benefits not only scholastic endeavors, but also practice beyond the academy.

We believe that conversations about explicit (rather than implicit) student learning objectives, course goals, and curricular strategies are an effective way of moving the enterprise of educating future designers forward. In terms of online content, we have learned that online "lectures" should be shorter and more numerous as opposed to the typical forty-five-to-fifty-minute oration in a face-to-face format. We have learned to celebrate our course management system by leveraging both its shortcomings and strengths. Course evaluations from early days of the process indicated students were struggling with content due to their inability to understand how to access it. As an electronic calendar was put in place, the number of comments decreased significantly. This fine-tuning resulted in greater satisfaction in the courses. Finally, we place a high priority on keeping track of details such as logistics and liabilities, copyright issues, university information technology parameters, metadata, and more. As we do so, we remember that librarians have intimate knowledge in many of these areas and will help with their implementation to make an online foray into education of twenty-first-century learners an unmitigated success.

Acknowledgements

These experiences with digital and physical approaches to hybrid teaching and learning were made possible by capitalizing on opportunities and offerings of university grants, people, offices, and equipment. For instance, faculty in our school made significant use of the e-Learning Innovation Initiative (eLii) internal grant in three sequential years to transform a single course, followed by a course sequence, and then to foster programmatic change through the creation of the Design Drive. Under these grants, our faculty developed lectures for online delivery in the Faculty Media Depot recording studio, fashioned supplementary websites on specific aspects of design, and curated blogs and other online content for a wide variety of courses and student populations to access throughout their undergraduate years. As part of the scaffolded and hybrid pedagogical approach, three faculty members participated in learning communities to help support and facilitate this educational experience. Bringing an even broader perspective to learning, three faculty members also participated in the university's Quality Enhancement Program on multimodal learning (mandated by accreditation requirements). To align hybrid instruction with concerns over rising textbook prices, two faculty members received support from an alternative textbook program to consider ways of providing and implementing student access to open educational resources (OERs).

Notes

1. Allison King, "From Sage on the Stage to Guide on the Side," *College Teaching* 41, no. 1 (1993): 30–35.
2. Tim Brown, *Design Thinking* (blog), accessed March 9, 2018, https://designthinking.ideo.com.
3. "Universal Design For Learning," Center for the Enhancement of Learning and Teaching (CELT), University of Kentucky, accessed March 7, 2018, http://www.uky.edu/celt/instructional-resources/getting-started/universal-design.
4. Benjamin S. Bloom, ed., *Taxonomy of Educational Objectives, Book I: Cognitive Domain* (White Plains, NY: Longman, 1956); A. H. Maslow, "A Theory of Human Motivation," *Psychological Review* 50 (1943): 370–96.

Other Works Consulted

Cret, Paul P. "The Ecole des Beaux-Arts and Architectural Education." *Journal of the American Society of Architectural Historians* 1, no. 2 (1941): 3–15.

Simon, Madlen. "The Beaux-Arts Atelier in America." In *84th ACSA Annual Meeting and Technology Conference Proceedings*. Edited by Judith Kinnard and Kenneth Schwartz, 319–25. Washington, DC: Association of Collegiate Schools of Architecture, 1996.

Chapter 4

Exploring the Development of Deeper Learning Skills

A Case Study Analysis of a Python E-learning Course

George Shaw, Jr.*

Many academic, public, and school libraries utilize online learning to deliver programs and library-related instruction. In many cases, these online learning sessions are used to provide information literacy or general library instruction. There are numerous ways in which the consumption of course content, a program, or specialized instruction conducted online is characterized. They can be referred to as online learning, internet learning, distributed learning, or distance education.[1]

According to Welsh and colleagues, e-learning can be defined as the use of network technology to provide educational instruction or information to an individual.[2] A broader approach to defining the term was undertaken in 2012, and many of the core elements, such as an approach to *teaching* and *learning* and communication to encourage interaction for new ways of *understanding and developing knowledge*, remain from early definitions of e-learning.[3] Libraries benefit from e-learning courses by reducing overhead cost, increasing the reach of services, and providing directed learning.[4]

Over the past few years, e-learning has become extremely important. Massive open online courses (MOOCs) have increased the availability and reach of excellent instruction. For example, Stanford University has a MOOC, free for anyone to take before close of course registration.[5] Coursera, FutureLearn, and OpenClassrooms are other popular examples of organizations that offer MOOCs. Within these types of online classrooms, there can be a diverse representation of students. While MOOCs have gained popularity over the past few years and will be the focus of this case study, the information gleaned from this chapter has implications for any e-learning course that involves the communication of information or knowledge to a group of students.

This case study will analyze an online Python development suite offered by the University of Michigan and explore how we use technology to engage students in deeper learning opportunities. The information gleaned from this case study will provide instruction librarians with additional insight regarding the technology they plan to integrate into their libraries and evaluating that technology so students gain optimal benefit from the instruction.

* **George Shaw, Jr.**, is a fourth-year doctoral student in the School of Library and Information Science (SLIS) at the University of South Carolina. Shaw's current doctoral research focuses on the intersection of computational science and public health. His research utilizes machine learning and text-mining methods to glean latent topics from Twitter regarding obesity to assist public health professionals with addressing obesity and other related chronic health conditions. When he is not in the doctoral "digs" working on his research, Shaw enjoys spending time with his family members and volunteering with Big Brothers Big Sisters of Greater Columbia.

Learning and Library Instruction

Understanding Deeper Learning

There has been increased emphasis within higher education for deeper learning approaches.[6] According to the 2017 New Media Consortium Horizon Report on emerging technology within education, deeper learning approaches within higher education pedagogy will become crucial to the learning process over the next several years. Deeper learning emphasizes that students should engage in higher order thinking (HOT) skills that include critical thinking and problem solving, collaboration, and self-directed learning to master the content.[7]

HOT skills are nonalgorithmic, tend to be complex, and require analyzing and synthesizing of the given content.[8] We should be careful and proceed with caution for students lacking these abilities.[9] In many MOOCs and asynchronous e-learning courses, students have to engage with the content, develop effective strategies to master the content, seek out additional sources, and be a part of the online community for that class.

Deeper learning and instructional technology are significantly intertwined when it comes to e-learning courses. According to the Association for Educational Communications and Technology (AECT), instructional technology is "the theory and practice of design, development, utilization, management, and evaluation of processes and resources for learning."[10] While it is important for students to engage in deep learning, instructional technology plays a vital role in this process as support.

Online Library Instruction

Whether academic, public, or school, librarians are being asked to do more with a limited amount of resources.[11] The expectation remains that library instruction will be good. This includes being course- and assignment-related; involving active learning and collaboration; appealing to multiple learning modalities; and providing learning with clear objectives.[12] Recent studies have used Dewald's work as an abstract framework to study the effectiveness of online information literacy instruction. Many of these studies have highlighted "that the most effective online information literacy learning objects include interactivity in the form of active learning."[13]

The concept of active learning in e-learning environments has impact for public, school, and special online library instruction. Active learning can be described as those activities that require analysis, synthesizing of concepts, and in-depth evaluation of the class content and the individuals' learning process. It is estimated that roughly 40 to 80 percent of students drop out of online courses.[14] Students benefit from online instruction that fosters collaboration with students and faculty members and involves a formative assessment of the learning process and knowledge acquisition based on formal tests or quizzes throughout the learning process.[15]

What Do We Want to Know?

This case study will analyze an online data science and python development suite offered through Coursera by the University of Michigan and explore the strategies they use to engage students in deeper learning opportunities. In addition to the content, the instructional technology that is employed for delivery of this course is extremely important. As an asynchronous course suite, interactivity and content engagement becomes vital for success.[16] In addition, learning new software programs and using the interface of the learning system in Coursera presents a student with its own set of challenges.

Learning a new programming language requires an extensive amount of time and active learning. For novice unexperienced programmers, grasping the terminology alone can be seen as a major accomplishment. It requires a shift in logic and conceptual understanding of variables and binary approaches to answering questions. The research questions this case study seeks to address are:

- How are aspects of deeper learning incorporated in an e-learning computational programming course?
- What are the implications from this analysis for online library instruction?

By the conclusion of this chapter, you will be presented with essential themes to evaluate your own e-learning environment and the utilization of deeper learning approaches from the lens of a computational science designed e-learning course.

The Research

The case study method for this research project uses a single instrument case study, exploratory approach to identify the themes that will be derived from the study.[17] I conducted the project. Sources of evidence for this study include documentation, direct observation, and my own participant observation.[18] Documents included lecture transcripts, PowerPoint materials, and assigned readings. For this study, direct observation involved the interface of the learning module used. As the participant observer, I interacted with the functionalities and course content that assisted with the learning process.

Data Collection

The Applied Data Science and Python Specialization that is offered through Coursera by the University of Michigan contains five courses. Each course builds upon the previous course, and there is an expectation that students enrolled in this specialization suite have some previous experience with programming. This case study uses the introductory course as the unit of analysis. It is imperative that aspects of the introductory course keep students engaged and assist with creating deeper learning opportunities, which require more discipline by the students.[19]

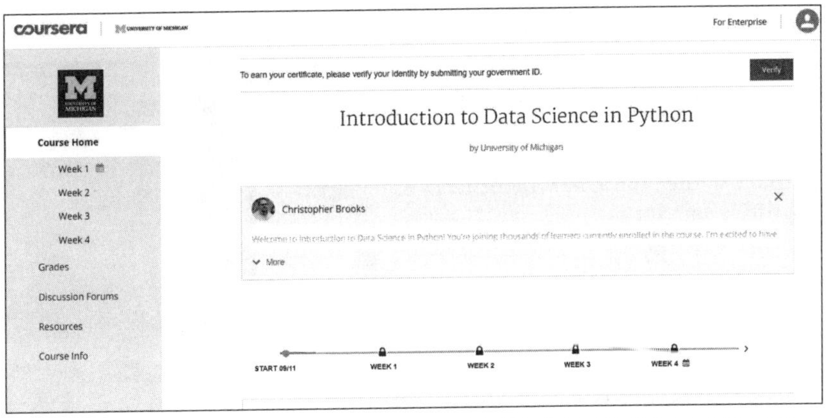

Figure 3.1
Screenshot of the Introduction to Data Science in Python course.

Documents Used for Analysis

There are multiple interpretations of what is considered a document, and this argument has been discussed in detail with regard to the contemporary meaning of this word (see Buckland's 1997 article "What Is a 'Document'?").[20] However, this is not an attempt to define documents but to describe the artifacts that were included as documents and the justification for this decision. PowerPoint presentations, the assigned course readings, discussion forums, linked tutorials, lecture transcripts, Python coding information, and general text describing the aforementioned artifacts were labeled as documents. These documents also supported students enrolled in the course who require closed-captioning for disability-related reasons.

Direct Observation

Direct observation was concerned with the physical layout of the learning module and the interaction with the interface (figure 3.1). The left navigational panel provided the user with access to the weekly course material (figure 3.2) and additional information that was necessary for the course. An interesting feature offered here was the opportunity to translate subtitles for the course. While it may seem insignificant, this is very important when you have international students enrolled in your e-learning course. Not only does this assist them in the learning process, it also addresses the needs for community members that are differently abled and those that speak English as a second language. The homepage interface also provided a completion bar. Research has shown the benefits of incorporating a progress indicator when completing tasks.[21]

Discussion

The discussion will focus on three themes identified that are essential to deeper learning—critical thinking, communication, and self-directed learning[22]—and an unrelated concept of interaction. While the themes discovered are important, the conversation in this section will focus on the relationship that they have with conducting online library instruction. In case study research, a strategy to identify meaning from abstract concepts and variables is identifying the relationships that exist to develop a coherent understanding of the data.[23]

Critical Thinking

As a novice Python programmer and participant observer, I used critical thinking to understand the terminology used in the course, think abstractly regarding problems that were presented, and evaluate the documents that were used to answer questions. With many library instruction courses, there is an assumption that students have basic to no level of understanding with regard to database use, concepts of information literacy, and understanding of information-literate transferable skills. Critical thinking in the e-learning environment will depend largely on the supporting documents. They not only provide contextual information to continue the cognitive processing from the lectures, but they also provide a sense of support for information that is unclear. The supporting resources were intricate in this process.

For students enrolled in e-learning library courses, online journal notes can provide the library instructor with insight into the learning process of students enrolled in the course. Once a student's preferred learning type is identified, it is necessary for librarians to develop personalized learning paths or suggested learning paths based on it. As noted, librarians are asked to do more with less. Customizable learning plans may be overreaching based on time constraints, but enough data generated can assist with generating categories of learners and provide predesigned learning paths as the librarian identifies cognitive barriers.

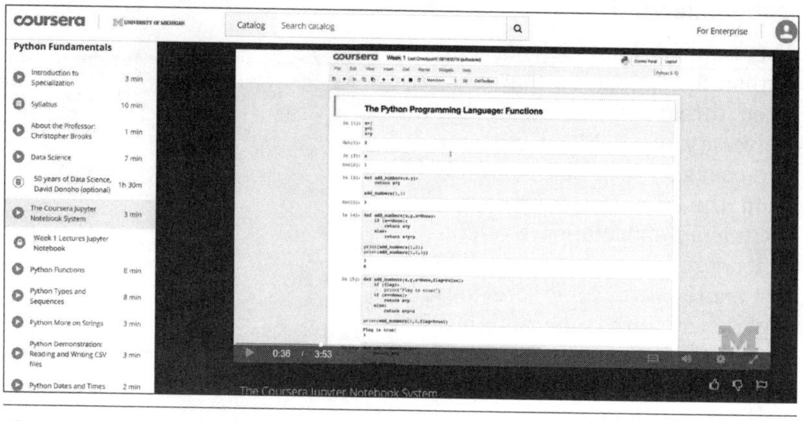

Figure 3.2
Screenshot of weekly module.

Communication

Outside the conversations that took place within the threads in the discussion area, there was minimal communication among students and the faculty instructor of the course. It is understandable, based on the number of students enrolled in this type of course, that communicating with hundreds of students can be difficult in this environment. From a participant point of view, communication was an essential element lost when compared to the face-to-face classroom. There were no emails, inbox notifications, or "checking-in" communication from the faculty instructor and course assistants.

Communication is handled differently, depending on how the library e-learning is constructed. Real-time communication during library instruction can be limited for asynchronous courses. Outside the context of emails, recorded lectures, and the learning management system communication tools, there is no direct communication with the instructor or other students. The issue with this form of communication is that text interpretation is up to the receiver. Therefore, when designing communication in this environment, it may be useful to integrate audio drop box features for students to communicate. Another user element is adding social media functionalities in the asynchronous course. What you choose is based on the technological support, integration, and interoperability of the current technology in place. One presentation at a recent Blended Learning in the Liberal Arts conference at Bryn Mawr College demonstrated how social media influence tools could assist with communication and assessing students' cognitive progression in class.[24]

With synchronous e-learning, real-time feedback is provided, whether that is the use of whiteboard space, verbal communication during a class session, or the use of application sharing. However, when you have hundreds of students in your course, virtual breakout rooms may provide an additional method for communication that reinforces the concepts and discussion from the lecture. Use of such virtual rooms also allows you to let these groups be student-led and provides students with directed-learning opportunities. Creating these spaces for students to use when library instruction is given as a one-time interaction provides a cost-effective way to continue the conversation after the library instruction. However, the design, management, and technical functions of this virtual environment will depend on a number of factors.

Self-Directed Learning

One factor that I underestimated as the participant observer was the degree of self-directed learning that was involved with this course. Since the lectures were prerecorded and there was significant reliance on the documents, a student had to seek additional information to understand or simplify convoluted concepts. Self-directed learning required a significant amount of motivation and clarification of "What I am learning?" and "How do I learn?"

When a student enrolls in an e-learning course, the questions "Why am I learning this?" and "From whom I am learning it?" are addressed by the course objectives or defined within the syllabus. Students have to continuously evaluate what they are learning and understand how they learn within the e-learning environment. As part of self-directed learning, students encountering difficulty may need system-imposed measures to help with self-efficacy. Library instruction aimed at addressing self-directed learning may require recognizing motivation factors, such as clear direction and reward or recognition.[25]

Interaction

Consistent with previous conversations, interaction pays an important role.[26] There were limited opportunities for interaction with classmates, the faculty instructor, and course assistants. While significant interaction was available with the course documents, there was a decrease in motivation to engage in significant deep learning that occurred during my tenure in the course. Moreover, limited communication further contributed to this low level of interaction.

The low level of interaction coupled with decreased motivation can be difficult to correct. As the participant observer, I found significant gaps between accesses of the course content. Critical thinking became less of a priority, and the completion of tasks with no in-depth engagement was the focus. It was apparent from my observation that the zeal for learning diminished and the completion of the course was now important.

Whether using a synchronous or an asynchronous e-learning environment, it will be critical for instructional librarians to keep students engaged. Conducting informal assessments, developing and maintaining good rapport with students, and continuously identifying the benefits as you move through topics or during a one-stop session are possible methods of maintaining motivation.

Conclusion

Many institutions have identified the critical role e-learning courses will play in the future. As budgets shrink for governmentally funded organizations, as learners require more mobility in their academic pursuits, and as e-learning courses try to meet the needs of the differently abled community, e-learning approaches and barriers will continue to be a topic of conversation. MOOCs and other forms of e-learning structures are addressing these demands, but it is imperative that the ability for students to engage in deep learning not be subdued by the change in delivery of quality education.

This case study allows us to identify themes that should be considered based on the documents that were scrutinized in the unit of analysis. The case study identified and provided insight into an interpretable understanding of important aspects of e-learning. Critical thinking, communication, self-directed learning, and interaction are evolving concepts that must be key elements in the online course design. External factors, such as policy and technology, will slightly shift how these concepts are defined, but the concepts will remain important if students or learners of online courses engage in deep learning.

While this was a single-case analysis that was exploratory in nature, using a multiple-case approach with a theoretical framework may provide additional or alternate perspectives. Also, this study should be compared with your organization's supported e-learning courses. Coursera and similarly related courses do not have the same level of rigor and evaluation when it comes to learning objectives, observance of the learning outcomes, and emphasis on Quality Matters accessibility standards for online learning. Lastly, the case study was directed toward one course in a suite of five. It would be beneficial to identify whether similar themes derive from the more advanced courses.

Notes

1. "What Is eLearning?" eLearningNC.gov, accessed March 7, 2018, www.elearningnc.gov/about_elearning/what_is_elearning/.
2. Elizabeth T. Welsh, Connie R. Wanberg, Kenneth G. Brown, and Marcia J. Simmering, "E-learning: Emerging Uses, Empirical Results and Future Directions," *International Journal of Training and Development* 7, no. 4 (2003): 246.
3. Albert Sangrà, Dimitrios Vlachopoulos, and Nati Cabrera, "Building an Inclusive Definition of E-learning: An Approach to the Conceptual Framework," *International Review of Research in Open and Distributed Learning* 13, no. 2 (2012): 145–59.
4. Sarah Chesemore, Rachel Van Noord, Janet Salm, and Cynthia Saletrik, *Trends in E-learning for Library Staff: A Summary of Research Findings* (Dublin, OH: OCLC, 2006), https://www.webjunction.org/content/dam/WebJunction/Documents/webJunction/Trends-in-E-Learning-for-Library-Staff.pdf.
5. John W. Moravec, "The University as a Flag of Convenience," Education Futures, December 13, 2011, http://www.educationfutures.com/2011/12/13/the-university-as-a-flag-of-convenience/.
6. "Deeper Learning Approaches," New Media Consortium, accessed March 7, 2018, https://www.nmc.org/horizon_topic/shift-to-deep-learning-approaches/.
7. S. Adams Becker, M. Cummins, A. Davis, A. Freeman, C. Hall Giesinger, and V. Ananthanarayanan, *NMC Horizon Report: 2017 Higher Education Edition* (Austin, TX: New Media Consortium, 2017).
8. Lauren B. Resnick, *Education and Learning to Think* (Washington, DC: National Academies Press, 1987); Lauren B. Resnick and D. P. Resnick, "Assessing the Thinking Curriculum: New Tools for Educational Reform," in *Changing Assessments: Alternative Views of Aptitude, Achievement and Instruction,* ed. Bernard R. Gifford and Mary Catherine O'Connor (Boston: Kluwer, 1992), 37–75.
9. Anat Zohar and Yehudit J. Dori, "Higher Order Thinking Skills and Low-Achieving Students: Are They Mutually Exclusive?" *Journal of the Learning Sciences* 12, no. 2 (2003): 145–81.
10. "What Is Knowledge Base?" Association for Educational Communications and Technology, 2001, accessed December 1, 2017, https://www.aect.org/standards/knowledgebase.html (page discontinued).
11. Amy Hall and Sarah Leeman, "Scaling Up: Rebuilding an Instruction Program with Limited Resources" (PowerPoint slides, webinar, Consortium of Academic and Research Libraries in Illinois [CARLI], December 7, 2016), https://www.carli.illinois.edu/products-services/pub-serv/instruction/ScalingUp-HallLeeman.
12. Nancy H. Dewald, "Transporting Good Library Instruction Practices into the Web Environment: An Analysis of Online Tutorials," *Journal of Academic Librarianship* 25, no. 1 (1999): 26–31.
13. Katie Greer, Amanda Nichols Hess, and Elizabeth W.

Kraemer, "The Librarian Leading the Machine: A Reassessment of Library Instruction Methods," *College and Research Libraries* 77, no. 3 (2016): 259.
14. Belinda G. Smith, "E-learning Technologies: A Comparative Study of Adult Learners Enrolled on Blended and Online Campuses Engaging in a Virtual Classroom" (doctoral dissertation, Capella University, 2010), ProQuest Dissertations and Theses database.
15. Greer, Hess, and Kraemer, "Librarian Leading the Machine"; Marcie Lynne Jacklin and Keely Robinson, "Evolution of Various Library Instruction Strategies: Using Student Feedback to Create and Enhance Online Active Learning Assignments," *Partnership: The Canadian Journal of Library and Information Practice and Research* 8, no. 1 (2013), www.criticalimprov.com/index.php/perj/issue/view/155.
16. Chesemore et al., "Trends in E-learning for Library Staff."
17. Robert K. Yin, *Applications of Case Study Research,* 2nd ed., Applied Social Research Methods Series, vol. 34 (Los Angeles: Sage, 2002); Robert K. Yin, *Case Study Research Design and Methods,* Applied Social Research Methods Series, vol. 5 (Los Angeles: Sage, 2002).
18. Yin, *Applications of Case Study Research*; Yin, *Case Study Research Design and Methods.*
19. Brian Burnsed, "Curtailing Dropouts at Online Universities," *US News and World Report,* October 20, 2010, https://www.usnews.com/education/online-education/articles/2010/10/20/curtailing-dropouts-at-online-universities.
20. Michael K. Buckland, "What is a 'Document'?" *Journal of the American Society for Information Science* 48, no. 9 (1997): 804.
21. Frederick G. Conrad, Mick P. Couper, Roger Tourangeau, and Andy Peytchev, "The Impact of Progress Indicators on Task Completion," *Interacting with Computers* 22, no. 5 (2010): 417–27.
22. Adams Becker et al., *NMC Horizon Report.*
23. Donna M. Zucker, "How to Do Case Study Research," in *Teaching Research Methods in the Humanities and Social Sciences,* ed. Mark Garner, Claire Wagner, and Barbara Kawulich (Famham, UK: Ashgate, 2009), 171–82, accessed from http://scholarworks.umass.edu/nursing_faculty_pubs/2.
24. Laura Zaylea, Tamara Sniad, and Kyle Harris, "Our Favorites! Tech Tools for Engagement in and beyond the Classroom" (presentation, Blended Learning in the Liberal Arts Conference, Bryn Mawr College, Bryn Mawr, PA, May 17–28, 2017).
25. Kris M. Y. Law, Victor C. S. Lee, and Y. T. Yu, "Learning Motivation in E-learning Facilitated Computer Programming Courses," *Computers and Education* 55, no. 1 (August 2010): 218–28.
26. Chesemore et al., "Trends in E-learning for Library Staff."

Chapter 5

Scanning Print to PDF

Opportunities and Obstacles for Screen Reader Accessibility

Robert Browder*

Scanning print to PDF opens a world of opportunity for sharing, using, and reusing resource materials. Here at Virginia Tech's Newman Library, we've been able to bring previously unavailable publications to the web in PDF format, including out-of-print journals and historical documents. Making resources available online in an accessible format creates opportunities for patrons that were not there before. Patrons can have their own copy of a document at the touch of button. After being rendered as an accessible PDF, resources that previously existed only in print take on new utility; they can be read aloud by a computer. This is a wonderful opportunity for all patrons, but especially for those with visual impairments.

How is it that PDF has remained so popular with the emergence and maturity of other digital reading technologies? In 2008, following many years of practical use and popularity, Adobe Systems, creator of the PDF file format, released the file specification to the International Organization for Standardization (ISO) for management and expansion.[1] Adobe did this in response to heavy use of the format by governments and public organizations. Releasing the specification to the ISO brought the PDF format into the world of "open technology" and cemented the confidence of public institutions. For the typical user, PDF provides a reading experience that is "near-book" by providing an application interface that creates a firm boundary from all the distraction that is the modern web browsing experience. With the combination of focus and flexibility provided by PDF format, it's really no wonder that it continues to thrive.

The ability to use semi-automated processes to create PDF documents from printed materials has obvious time-saving advantages. With the right equipment, you can scan fifty to ninety printed pages per minute. However, merely scanning printed materials as images is not enough. While creating a digital image of text on a page is a great leap in preservation and "sharability," a wide variety of vision issues may affect any of us at some point in our lives, rendering visually oriented materials difficult or impossible to use. Making PDF documents accessible to those with visual disabilities via screen reader technology is well within the reach of our current technical abilities. However, scanning print to PDF is not a panacea to create accessibility for all types of content. While it is perfect for some types of content, more complex types of content prove to be remarkably difficult and time-consuming to render screen-reader-accessible in PDF.

Scanning print to PDF presents unique opportunities and challenges. The source material to be scanned will determine how much effort is required to make a PDF accessible. For complex content like large tables, graphs, charts, and equations, HTML often provides better opportunities for accessibility and production efficiency than is possible with PDF. For simpler content, such as text and images that can be described with ease verbally, scanning print to PDF is often the most streamlined approach to creating an accessible resource from printed materials. In nearly all cases,

* **Robert Browder** is a digital publishing specialist with VT Publishing, a service of Virginia Tech Libraries. Since obtaining his undergraduate degree in information science and systems in 2011 from Radford University, Browder has served in a variety of technology and publishing roles. His work currently focuses on managing resources and workflows associated with the publication of online open-access scholarly journals.

PDF makes a suitable "pass-through" and preservation format to bring print into digital format while avoiding manual transcription processes.

Understanding Visual Disability

When we think about *visual disability* as a general term, we are addressing a community of conditions that have different causes but often share similar functional limitations. Visual impairment includes everything from complete blindness to conditions that merely require corrective lenses. Conditions like low vision, color-blindness, and corneal opacities each have their own limitations.

The World Health Organization groups moderate to severe vision impairment under the term *low vision*.[2] The majority of conditions categorized as low vision can be improved with the use of corrective lens. However, in the absence of corrective lens, low vision can make it incredibly difficult for individuals to read and perform daily tasks.

Color-blindness results in perceptions of colors that differ from the way the majority of the population perceive them. Three forms of color blindness are currently documented: red appears as green, blue appears as yellow, and complete absence of color vision. According to the National Eye Institute, "As many as 8 percent of men and 0.5 percent of women with Northern European ancestry have the common form of red-green color blindness."[3] As you might imagine, color-blindness creates unique challenges for interpreting color-coded information.

Globally, most cases of blindness can fit within a few categories. Corneal opacities (CO), clouding of the cornea, are often the result of infections but can also result from injury. Age-related macular degeneration is a progressive degeneration of a person's main field of vision due to lesions of the retina. Glaucoma is caused by optic neuropathy, in which messages from the eye are either not conducted or poorly conducted to the brain. Cataract is a clouding of the lens that prevents light from entering the eye.[4]

The World Health Organization reports that 253 million people live with visual impairment of some kind.[5] While creating accessible digital materials does not solve the root problem, it does make information available to those who otherwise would not have it. Consider the benefit you get from reading an article you are interested in and multiply it by 253 million. That's real opportunity there.

The Scanning Process

Scanning print to PDF is a process that is used regularly at Virginia Tech's University Libraries. The scanning process is the heart of our print-to-PDF pipeline. Combined with a reliable optical character recognition (OCR) process, automated scanning provides extraordinary efficiency. Christy Stanley, Virginia Tech University Libraries scanning specialist, uses a process consisting of the following basic steps:

- Prepare for automated feed scanning
  - Organization of materials
  - Removal of spine for bound materials
- Scanning
  - Loading and monitoring the scanner
- Adjust scanned pages
  - Adjust for skew
  - Crop pages to remove ragged edges
- Compile scanned pages into PDF documents
- Color balance adjustments
  - Setting the text to black makes it much more legible for those with low vision and may improve the quality of OCR output.
- OCR
  - This step can be done either at the end of the scanning process or at the beginning of the read order editing process.

We have a couple of Fujitsu scanners, the 6240-Z and the 6770. Both have an auto-feed tray and a flatbed. The 6770 will handle larger pages and will scan more pages per minute. There are lots of options for scanners made by familiar brands like Kodak, Canon, and HP that provide functionality similar to these. If you're thinking about buying a scanner and your library is already invested in equipment from a particular vendor, it may make sense to get their stuff in the hope that all components will play together nicely. Most scanners come with software that may be helpful in building or refining the scanning process.

After pages are scanned, post-processing can be achieved using vendor software that came with the scanner or an open-source tool like Scan Tailor. Post-processing allows the technician to straighten crooked pages, adjust the color balance, remove unsightly edges, and group a collection of scanned pages into a single PDF document.

The importance of adjusting the color balance of a document should not be ignored. Color balance adjustments can often increase color contrast of typography, yielding notable improvements in readability for those with low vision. OCR processes may also benefit from color balance adjustments.

Color can be an important part of any visual communication and can a have serious impact on accessibility. Color contrast is important for users with low vision or color blindness. Color is often used to convey meaning and communicate essential information. Nowhere do we see this more clearly than in the example of charts and graphs. Colors without appropriate contrast may render bar graphs and charts difficult to use. This situation must be considered carefully when scanning documents that contain graphics that use color to communicate. Alternative text (alt text) can be used to add meaning to images that have poor color contrast.

Setting Expectations for Output of the Optical Character Recognition Process

OCR is a process that uses computer algorithms to analyze and identify letter shapes and words. OCR can be achieved with Adobe Acrobat or, in some cases, with software that came with the scanner. An OCR process adds character encoding to the document so that screen readers can read the document to users with visual impairments. OCR also allows users to copy and paste text from the document. While current OCR technologies do pretty well with recognizing standard fonts, OCR algorithms will be confounded by poor quality scans, decorative typefaces, and handwriting. So the output of an OCR process can be only as good as the input. Keep this in mind when setting expectations for print-to-PDF projects.

Testing the Output

After OCR, the document must be tested. A screen reader such as JAWS, NVDA, or VoiceOver will be very useful. Adobe Acrobat will also prove indispensable. Using screen readers allows us to know something about the experience the document will provide to those with visual impairments. Using Acrobat will provide us with a window into the technical organization of the scanned document.

As a first step, it is always useful to test the document with a screen reader. Listen carefully as the application reads the text to you. Pay attention and make note of any inconsistencies. Since this document is newly scanned, we can expect that some content, such as images or other graphics, will be skipped over by the screen reader. We may also find that content is not always read in the correct order. We may find that artifacts of the document, such as running headers or footers, are read by the application when they should not be. While the scanning and OCR processes have saved a great deal of time, we may find that the resulting screen reader output is intelligible but not intelligent. Human intervention is typically required to organize the document in such a way that its full context can be conveyed via screen reader.

Abode Acrobat provides tools that can be used to analyze and edit the underlying structure of PDF documents. Developing familiarity with this tool kit is a marathon, not a sprint. Consistent time investment in developing skills with this tool set will yield best results. Acrobat offers various levels of automation for different tasks that are helpful in creating accessible documents, including tagging, accessibility checking, alternative text, and reading order.

Tagging PDF Documents

One of the most important steps in creating accessible PDF documents is tagging. Tagging allows us to define different elements within the document. Common elements that need to be tagged are headings, paragraphs, and images. Screen readers use these tags to assist the reader in using and navigating the document. Acrobat provides automation for this task that is marginally helpful. The automated process will often tag artifacts that should be ignored by the screen reader. Quality will be improved with manual review and editing.

Alternative Text for Images, Figures, Graphs, and Charts

Alternative text is descriptive text that can be added to a document to replace images, figures, math, graphs, and charts when the document is read by a screen reader. Alt text fills in the blanks that otherwise result from unseen images. How well alt text fills in those blanks is another story. Ideally, alt text would be supplied by the author of a text, but in the case of scanning, this is usually impossible. Alt text must be created by someone who understands the context and content of the images. With simple images and figures, filling in the alt text is a simple task. With complex charts and graphs, creating alt text that reliably communicates the information becomes a specialty that may require a subject specialist.

While alt text is intended to create an experience that is comparable to interacting with the document visually, whether or not it actually does is, in many cases, debatable. HTML is often a better format for complex graphs and charts. Tactile graphics can create a truly comparable experience for the visually impaired.

Read Order Editing

Read order is the order in which a screen reader will read the contents of a PDF to a human listener. While a human reader will evaluate a page using visual cues, a screen reader needs to have the read order explicitly defined. Acrobat can automate the process of assigning read order to a PDF document. But it cannot determine which elements add meaning to the work or the correct reading order for content found in complex layouts. Ideally, read order should be comparable to the way a human would read a text.

For example, let's consider a typical page that contains a running header in the top right corner of the page with page number and several paragraphs of text in the body of the page. Even with just these few elements on the page, there is possibility for improperly assigned read order to disrupt the flow of the text and its meaning. Let's suppose that an automated read order assignment has defined the running header as the first element on the page and the paragraphs in the body text as the second, third, and fourth elements. At first glance this may seem fine, but what if the first sentence on the page is a continuation of the last sentence on the previous page? If the screen reader reads the running header first, it will break the flow of the sentence and possibly confuse or distort its meaning. This is a serious quality issue that can create problems for users of the resource. The solution to this problem is to manually edit the read order of the document. The correct action in this case would be to define all of the running headers with page numbers throughout the entire document as background and assign the first paragraph in the body text as the first element on the page. This approach maintains the flow and meaning of the content.

Tables

Tables are a special challenge for the print-to-PDF process. Simple tables are easy enough to tag and use with a screen reader. The simplest of tables can even be tagged as a figure and amply described with alt text. Larger tables are challenging and time-consuming to tag in PDF. I argue that even the most detailed tagged tables do not provide a comparable experience for those with visual impairments. Let's take a moment to remember what a table is and what it is supposed to do. A table is a tool that creates a matrix that allows the user to explore data relationships in a two-dimensional format, columns and rows. The matrix functionality that makes a table such a valuable tool for presenting information can be severely diminished by representing it verbally. Trends and patterns that are obvious when using the table either visually or tactilely may be much more difficult to identify when attempting to explore the information verbally. The goal is to share information revealed by looking at the relationships of data organized within the matrix. HTML, braille, and tactile graphics are often better formats for this type of complex content.

What about Math?

While an OCR process can interpret characters and group them into words and sentences, generating a consistent screen reader experience for mathematical equations is a bit beyond what can reasonably be expected from the OCR process. If equations are included as part of a sentence, they may or may not come through reliably. In the case that equations are presented on their own apart from the text, they can be tagged as figures and have a verbal description added as alt text. This approach is especially helpful with complex multilevel equations that use special characters and symbols, such as Greek letters.

Tagging equations as figures and adding alt text is a reasonable way to treat equations in the print-to-PDF process; however, it raises another issue. The alt text must be *meaningful*. A subject specialist who understands how to correctly communicate the equation with a text description will be required.

Opportunity or Obstacle? It's All about the Content

While scanning print to PDF is a great opportunity for preserving and sharing printed materials of all types over the web and is a great entry point for bringing print into the digital space, the ability to produce a PDF that is highly accessible for screen readers is not always straightforward and often requires excessive inputs of time and specialized skills. The complexity of content in the source material is the deciding factor in how well a PDF document can meet the rigorous demands of screen reader accessibility. PDF offers wonderful opportunities for plain text and images. We start to run into obstacles when documents contain more complex types of content like tables, graphs, and complex math equations. While all of these content types perform fine visually, developing the PDF document to the point that it provides a comparable experience delivered verbally via screen reader is time-consuming and often requires input of specialized skills.

To Scan or Not to Scan?

Yes, by all means, scan. But know your goals, know the limitations of a print-to-PDF scanning process, and set expectations accordingly. PDF readily satisfies goals for preservation and dissemination of visually accessibly materials. PDF also performs well as a pass-through format to aid in avoiding manual transcription. PDF can sometimes satisfy the needs of accessible documents, depending on the types of content found in the document. Before a scanning project begins, it is important to consider whether or not the complexity of the content can be faithfully communicated via PDF with screen reader technology and how much effort will be required to organize PDF documents for screen reader accessibility.

Notes

1. "PDF Format Becomes ISO Standard," International Standards Organization, July 2, 2008, https://www.iso.org/news/2008/07/Ref1141.html.
2. "Vision Impairment and Blindness," fact sheet, World Health Organization, last updated October 2017, www.who.int/mediacentre/factsheets/fs282/en/.
3. "Facts about Color Blindness," National Eye Institute, National Institutes of Health, last updated February 2015, https://nei.nih.gov/health/color_blindness/facts_about.
4. "Priority Eye Diseases," World Health Organization, accessed March 8, 2018, www.who.int/blindness/causes/priority/en/index8.html.
5. "Vision Impairment and Blindness."

Chapter 6

Big Impact with littleBits

Stacy Brown*

A library of any type is a place to learn for all students. In most libraries, students originate from diverse cultures, have different educational needs and experiences, possess a range of social and emotional distinctions, and represent a variety of ages. The American Library Association's *Strategic Directions* notes equitable access as a key action area for libraries of the future.[1] Specifically, its strategic plan notes the need to accommodate individuals with language barriers, physical barriers, barriers to equal education, religious differences, and more. As a result, librarians are faced with the challenge of leveraging their resources to accommodate a variety of cognitive differences while accounting for physical differences. Discovering technology that is accessible to all and that can provide value to a diverse population can be challenging. In our school library, when we acquired littleBits, we also acquired a positive approach to integrating technology across a diverse set of needs.

LittleBits are small magnetic circuits that snap together to allow users to create simple inventions, such as providing a source of light, and more complex inventions, like creating a mobile underwater aquarium scene. LittleBits can be purchased as individual kits or within different types of specific kits. Some bits are more advanced than others. The blue bit represents the power source and connects to a 9-volt battery with a battery cable that is included. Pink bits represent input bits, allowing the creator to control the circuit. Examples include a dimmer switch, a button, or a pulse. Green bits represent output bits and accomplish a specific task. Examples of these include LEDs generating light, servos causing motion, or buzzers creating sound. Because littleBits can generate sound, light (flashing or continuous), and movement, they can accommodate individuals who are visually impaired or have hearing loss. Additionally, because input bits can control the intensity of the output components, students with sensory processing disorders can control the output of sound, light, or movement, making littleBits accessible for students with specific sensory needs. Finally, the orange bits are considered to be accessory bits that allow the user to extend the circuit with the use of branches as well as add levels of complexity to the circuits. With these bits, students with limitations in mobility range can still build with littleBits. With the inclusion of the wire bit, the circuits can extend to allow for a more expansive work area also allowing for a wider range of motion. The wireless transmitter and wireless receiver bits work together to allow the creation of a circuit that can be controlled remotely, which also extends the accessibility. The benefits of working with littleBits technology are extensive.

Instruction with littleBits can be differentiated to accommodate a variety of age groups and skill levels. Four- and five-year-olds can create simple inventions using only three bits. For example, our kindergarten students were learning about zoo animals. As a fun design challenge, we created design challenge cards related to the theme of zoo animals for the students to solve in small groups. With the students working in

* **Stacy Brown** is the 21st Century Learning Coordinator at the Davis Academy in Atlanta, Georgia, where she manages two media centers in a kindergarten prep through eighth grade academic environment. Recognized for facilitating the integration of technology into the curriculum, she leads #MakerMonday for pre–K through fifth grade, teaches a fourth grade programming and robotics class, developed a fifth grade entrepreneurship and technology course, coordinates a student technology leadership program known as Network Sherpas, and leads teachers' professional development in the area of technology integration.

teams of two and three, design challenges included creating a device that the zookeeper can use to alert the zoo animals that it is their feeding time. Using the blue power bit, the pink button input bit, and the green buzzer output bit, the team of kindergarteners were able to build a contraption out of construction paper, popsicle sticks, and pipe cleaners to house their "feeder alert." Other examples included designing a cooling system for the pandas, creating a zoo animal that can move, or building a lion cage that lights up when the door is opened. This last challenge used four bits, including a light sensor, allowing the teacher to designate this challenge for students who needed an additional layer of complexity to enhance their learning.

Older students can also create with littleBits in ways that will challenge them. Facilitating more complex design challenges tailored to meet the time constraints of the students can provide rewarding learning opportunities. Students learn to be self-managers as they break down tasks and set their own deadlines to accomplish a larger task within a specific time frame. In the book *Empower*, the authors write that this is a critical component of project management.[2] Students are cultivating skills that will serve them well in a professional setting. Merging the learning with littleBits with the core curriculum is another added advantage. For example, fifth graders learning about Jewish customs can create menorahs, dreidels, and mezuzahs out of littleBits. Integrating Lego pieces can also add to the design process with the incorporation of different building materials. Determining which lights work best, such as long LEDs or short bright LEDs, and which pink input, such as a dimmer or a button, will provide the most effective control for lighting the menorah each night is just as important to the design process. Additionally, as students consider the target audience for their designs, they can learn a variety of ways to accommodate a diverse user group. For example, if they are developing a menorah for the visually impaired, incorporating a sound trigger so that the LED candles light up with the trigger of sound can make menorah lighting accessible to individuals with sight limitations. LittleBits not only can be used by those with different abilities but also can be used to create objects for individuals with different abilities. The dual functionality of littleBits results in a lesson in empathy as users are encouraged to consider accessibility in their product development.

Oftentimes when our students are working with littleBits, we refer to them as little engineers. Engineers typically construct to solve a problem. As Amy Wilson-Lopez and Stacie Gregory state in their article "Integrating Literacy and Engineering Instruction for Young Learners," linking children's literature to engineering "can align with students' interests; resonate with their linguistic, cultural, or geographic backgrounds; or introduce them to problems that they have witnessed in their homes or communities."[3] They give the example of having fifth graders read excerpts from the young adult book *Candy Bomber: The Story of the Berlin Airlift's "Chocolate Pilot"*[4] and having the students design a device that would have allowed the candy bomber to safely deliver candy to the hungry children in Germany. Literary connections can help bring the engineering challenges to life, mimicking the solution of real-world problems by students.

Adults can learn with littleBits too. We have incorporated littleBits into our professional development for teachers and have modeled the learning that happens at school for our parents as well. For teachers, understanding this process improves their teaching abilities while helping them to discover new ways to implement different technologies in their curriculum. As stated in the article "The Philosophy of Educational Makerspaces," it is crucial that the process of making remain learner-driven as opposed to teacher-driven.[5] With exposure, parents can also understand the value of this approach to learning as part of their child's education and, in turn, can support these efforts. Constructing with littleBits represents a form of maker education. Maker education can be viewed as a grassroots effort in response to one-size-fits-all education in which instruction is designed for the masses.[6] The accessibility of littleBits allows the learning to be customized.

Acquisition

At the Davis Academy, we started small. We began our littleBits journey with the purchase of one Pro Workshop set, allowing eighteen individuals working in groups of two to create at one time. From the beginning, we used social media platforms, such as Twitter, to send our inventions to the creators of littleBits so that they could see the innovative projects that our students were making. In 2015, littleBits launched a school chapter program, in which schools that applied and were accepted would have a landing page on the littleBits website to upload their inventions, participate in monthly challenges, and receive discounts on additional littleBits. Our school was accepted into this program, which is now known as the littleBits Inventor Club. Being a part of the Chapter Program/Inventor Club has provided valuable learning opportunities for our school. For example, students in a variety of grades participated in several monthly challenges, including creating a project inspired by Harry Potter, inventing a birthday-themed invention in celebration of littleBits' fifth birthday (figure 5.1), and inventing something that glows with littleBits. As a winner of one of the challenges, our school received the Rule Your Room kit from littleBits as a reward. We have been able to circulate this newest kit into our curriculum for fourth and fifth graders as part of their littleBits design challenge rotations.

Our school hosts Scholastic book fairs twice a year, and through the Scholastic dollars program, we are able to use a portion of the funds earned through our book fair to purchase items available in the Scholastic catalog. This catalog now offers littleBits, and as a result of successful book fairs, we were able to purchase two littleBits Synthesizer kits. With these acquisitions, the volume of projects that we create and their level of sophistication grew. Internally, our school has seen the value of this tool and how it is has enriched our learning community. As a result, we were able to include the littleBits Pro Library as part of our 2016–17 capital campaign. In our first two years of working with littleBits, acquiring the Pro Library seemed like a dream. Through consistent usage and demonstrated value of building this tool into our curriculum, we were able to gain the financial support to make this dream a reality.

Figure 5.1
Middle school students creating a birthday-inspired invention in honor of littleBits' fifth birthday.

Benefits of Bits

With the acquisition of an expanded library of littleBits, we have had the pleasure of strengthening collaboration, creativity, and the application of higher-order thinking skills. Students become problem solvers who persevere through the unknown. They become designers as they begin to understand the value of planning a well-organized blueprint for their creations. They become editors as they go back to alter their design plans to meet an unforeseen need. They become team players as they rely on each other's varying strengths and areas of expertise to complete a project on time. They become partners working toward a common goal that fuels their passions and interests.

Our school uses littleBits as part of a fourth grade exploratory class that meets three times a week for fifty minutes for nine weeks. Students have to meet their deadlines and ensure they have fulfilled the project goals. They have to work as part of a successful design team to meet their clients' needs. They are simulating the experience of real-world professionals working toward a common goal to earn a profit or, in their case, earn a respectable grade for their efforts. Students study characteristics that make engineers, designers, builders, architects, and artists desirable in the work force. With a clear understanding of these characteristics, they formulate interview questions for their classmates to help craft a successful design team. Once the interview process is complete, students are ready to form their teams and begin the brainstorming process to create their inventions with littleBits. Some inventions solve problems, and some are created for entertainment value. Through teamwork and collaboration, the design teams decide upon their goals and work together to successfully implement the design, create the prototype, and carry out the building process. In doing so, they are making social connections while learning to work with teammates who have strengths different from their own. Additionally, they are given a creative outlet to pursue their unique ideas and designs. Students are exposed to a new form of learning with their hands and, in turn, become experts in an area they had not previously explored.

Programming Possibilities

In collaborating with core subject teachers and other special teachers in the school community, students can leverage their knowledge of littleBits to show what they know in an array of subject areas. The programming possibilities are plentiful for all ages. Some activities can be very structured, whereas others can be intentionally more abstract. The time constraints can help dictate the facilitator's approach.

Setting up the time and the space for self-guided exploration and experimentation is rewarding as students can go at their own pace and pursue their own path. At the Davis Academy, we hosted a Bits Bar during our Maker Monday program in which littleBits were set out on a long counter or on top of a low book shelf, and students could come to the bar to put the bits together to make a variety of contraptions and explore how they work. This is a great activity for those without prior experience using littleBits. Selecting a broad theme, such as "Pick a Force," gives students a loose framework to work within but encourages creativity. With this theme, students design a contraption that generates energy to create physical movement. The theme is broad but has a clear objective. The opposite approach can also be taken, in which students are given a "Bucket of Bits" and with the littleBits provided are charged with creating something uniquely their own. Within the confines of the littleBits they are allotted, they can work in small groups to make an invention of their choosing.

In contrast, littleBits challenges can allow for more structured activities. For early morning brain

Figure 5.2
Middle school students creating a basketball game out of littleBits for the media center arcade.

warm-ups, fifth graders participated in littleBits challenges in which they were given an objective, the littleBits to accomplish the objective, and the craft supplies to go with it in one big bag. Challenges included the following: "New York City is known as the city that never sleeps. Design a skyscraper that includes a power button to light up the building so the light always shines." Another challenge was to invent a security device for a backpack. Using a battery as the power source, a light sensor, and a buzzer, students were able to create a device that was hidden inside a backpack and buzzed when exposed to light (or when a culprit was mysteriously attempting to take something out of the backpack). Our sixth graders participated in the Inventor Club's challenge to create a birthday-themed invention with littleBits in honor of the company's fifth birthday. One creation included a birthday cake that moved in a circular motion with lit candles on top made of LED lights. Third graders do an invention unit as part of their core curriculum and, as a result, we had students create their own inventions using littleBits to bring the learning to life. Seventh and eighth graders were tasked with turning the media center into an arcade for other students and faculty to enjoy. Using littleBits, students built a variety of games, such as a one entitled Goal Score Light, in which a light flashed when a goal was scored. This can be created using the motion trigger, an LED light bit, and the power source. The students can use cardboard to build the chute to work in conjunction with a small plastic ball. Another group created a basketball game with a launcher to launch the miniature basketball into the holes to earn points (figure 5.2).

Students of all ages can participate in rotational circuits using premade littleBits challenges in which specific littleBits are provided, the challenges are explained, and instructions are offered. The littleBits website, the Pinterest app or website, and the Teachers Pay Teachers website are all sources for premade littleBits challenge cards, or you can create your own challenge cards. With first graders, I set up a series of challenge cards and the littleBits required at different tables. Working in groups of three to four students, each team would use the magnetic littleBits to create simple circuits and then rotate to the next table to complete a different littleBits challenge within their group. This rotational setup allowed them exposure to a variety of littleBits, providing them with a broader understanding of how the different littleBits worked.

Conclusion

LittleBits makes it easy to reach learners at every level and at every age. There are a multitude of ways that littleBits can be integrated into the school library independent of other curriculum or as a catalyst to deepen the learning in a specified subject area. The vast number of littleBits available allows for significant differentiation across the population. Their ease of use, their compact size, and the flexibility of integrating other tangible items—such as Legos, cardboard, craft supplies, and more—allow users to differentiate the complexity of their creations. Since adopting littleBits in our school, we have witnessed the growth of student interest in exploring with educational technology. As we continue to infuse learning with littleBits into our school community, we continue to see the rewards for all students.

Notes

1. *American Library Association Strategic Directions* (Chicago: American Library Association, 2017), http://www.ala.org/aboutala/sites/ala.org.aboutala/files/content/governance/StrategicPlan/Strategic%20Directions%202017_Update.pdf.
2. John Spencer and A. J. Juliani, *Empower: What Happens When Students Own Their Learning* (IMPress, 2017), 84.
3. Amy Wilson-Lopez and Stacie Gregory, "Integrating Literacy and Engineering Instruction for Young Learners," *Reading Teacher* 69, no. 1 (July/August 2015): 27.
4. M. O. Tunnell, *Candy Bomber: The Story of the Berlin Airlift's "Chocolate Pilot"* (Watertown, MA: Charlesbridge, 2010).
5. R. Steven Kurti, Debby L. Kurti, and Laura Fleming, "The Philosophy of Educational Makerspaces: Part 1 of Making an Educational Makerspace," *Teacher Librarian* 41, no. 5 (June 2014): 8–11, Professional Development Collection, EBSCOhost.
6. Kurti, Kurti, and Fleming, "The Philosophy of Educational Makerspaces."

Chapter 7

Identifying and Removing Barriers

How Campus Partners Cultivate Diverse Online Learning Environments

Aisha S. Haynes*

Online courses are becoming increasingly popular in educational institutions. Enrollments in online college courses are growing at a rapid pace.[1] Online courses have the potential to attract students who may not be able to enroll in traditional face-to-face courses. As colleges and universities move toward offering more online courses, students with special needs may get left behind.[2] Universal design becomes more important every year as institutions of higher education extend their reach and course offerings to a variety of students near and far. Many students, including those students with disabilities, are opting for online versions of courses.

According to Tobin, Universal Design for Learning (UDL) is an educational framework for designing multiple ways for learners to interact, engage, and experience content.[3] UDL was initially developed to provide equal learning opportunities for students in traditional face-to-face courses, but the framework has been adapted for online courses. UDL goes beyond being helpful for students with disabilities. These principles often benefit all learners.

Online learning can present challenges for all students. If course accessibility and usability are not appropriately addressed, challenges can be particularly significant for students with various disabilities.[4] Some students may require unique support in the online learning environment, and many educators erroneously assume that all materials available online are accessible to all students. Oftentimes, faculty don't know how UDL strategies can benefit students.[5]

Overview of the University of South Carolina

USC–Columbia is a large, diverse public university with a Carnegie I research classification. The university is the state flagship institution, which encompasses many disciplines and schools, strong departmental structures, and a strong sense of faculty governance. The USC system includes three senior four-year campuses—USC–Aiken, USC–Upstate, and USC–Beaufort—which are governed by separate academic leadership. The system also includes four Palmetto College regional campuses (USC–Lancaster, USC–Salkehatchie, USC–Sumter, and USC–Union). The USC system enrollment exceeds 50,000 students—over 42,000 undergraduate students, 6,900 graduate students, and 1,800 professional students. The system employs more than 3,300 full-time faculty.[6]

In addition to traditional courses, USC–Columbia and the Palmetto College regional campuses have a wide array of distributed learning (DL) courses

* **Dr. Aisha S. Haynes** is the Program Manager for Distributed Learning at the Center for Teaching Excellence: University of South Carolina–Columbia. As program manager, she oversees the design, creation, and ongoing improvement of distributed learning (online and blended) delivery methods. Haynes' research interests include instructional design in online learning environments, online course accessibility, Universal Design for Learning, learning styles, and collaboration and engagement in online learning environments.

through many degree programs. USC uses the umbrella of DL to describe courses offered through a few modalities: 100 percent online, blended, and two-way video. Courses that are delivered 50 percent or more online, either synchronously or asynchronously, fall under DL.

University of South Carolina Libraries

The USC system is home to fourteen libraries. The University Libraries support learning and discovery by connecting university faculty, staff, and students with collections and support for research and teaching. Librarians collaborate with campus partners including departmental liaisons, the Office of Distributed Learning, and the Center for Teaching Excellence (CTE) to provide quality services for students who enroll in DL courses and faculty who teach DL courses.

University library staff assist faculty with addressing copyright concerns by utilizing e-reserves. Staff scan library materials for faculty and input the material in the content collection of the Blackboard learning management system. Librarians collaborate with the Student Disability Resource Center (SDRC) to create accessible scanned materials.

Instructors have the ability to include library resources within DL courses by linking to interactive subject guides where students can access pertinent course information. Librarians can create course guides for class research assignments. Faculty and students at a distance can request that journal articles and book chapters be scanned and provided electronically.

Best Practices in Online Learning

In 2000, USC introduced its first fully online course. Today, one undergraduate degree; forty-two graduate degrees, certificate programs, and specialist degrees; and seven online degree completion programs are offered through DL at the university. USC offers 1,343 DL courses, and the enrollments in DL courses was 27,879 in annual year 2017.

The CTE, as part of the Office of the Provost, inspires excellence and innovation in teaching. The center provides programming, resources, and opportunities that foster innovative and effective pedagogical practices among all who teach at USC–Columbia and the Palmetto College regional campuses. There are three instructional designers and one instructional developer at the CTE. Faculty receive grant money and assistance from instructional designers and the Division of Information Technology to design quality online courses in the grant program. The program was created to help get faculty interested in teaching online. One of the grantees had an interest in the Quality Matters (QM) program as part of the grant and helped the university become aware of the nationally known organization. The QM program is recognized as being a leader in quality assurance for online courses.[7]

Some ideas for best practices in online learning and accessibility, which instructors and professors can take away from sessions with the Center for Teaching Excellence include:

- Providing step-by-step instructions for accessing the course and all course materials. This can include an "orientation" or "getting started" module that orients the students with the Course Management System.
- Offering multiple formats of materials, including Word and PDF documents. Format the documents following established accessibility guidelines.
- Checking document accessibility (built-in accessibility checkers are available for Microsoft 2010 and 2013 products).
- Providing transcripts and closed captioning for all lectures, talks, and synchronous or asynchronous interactions with students.
- Using Sans Serif fonts (Arial, Calibri, among others) to increase visibility and accessibility. Font size for documents should be no less than 12 point and with presentations no less than 24 points.
- Using **bold** to display emphasis rather than color (doing so increases accessibility for students with color blindness).
- Maintaining ongoing one-on-one and group communication with students; establishing positive relationships with students and offering accessible opportunities for interaction.[8]

Distributed Learning Quality Review

During the 2012–13 academic year, the provost announced a DL quality review (DLQR) as part of the commitment to ensure high-quality online courses. A provost's committee on DL was created to assist with the process. The committee is faculty-driven and includes the Associate Provost and Director of Distributed Learning, representatives from the CTE, faculty, and other university staff who are leaders in DL on campus. The committee consists of several subcommittees. One subcommittee, the Best Practices and Quality Assurance Subcommittee, was tasked with creating or selecting best practices for the design of all online courses. The committee adopted the QM standards as a basis for quality review because they focus on course design. Some of the standards were modified to meet the needs of the university.

The general standards for the quality assurance document include course overview and introduction, learning outcomes or objectives, assessment and measurement, instructional materials, course activity and learner interaction, course technology, student support, usability, and accessibility. CTE instructional designers and staff from the SDRC collaborated to create in-house accessibility standards for all online courses. The accessibility standards include the following:

- Optical character recognition (OCR) has been performed on all PDF files before they are posted.
- PDF files are accompanied by their Word document equivalent or a link to the HTML equivalent.
- All posted documents (Word, Excel, PowerPoint, etc.) are accessible and usable by screen readers.
- Videos are captioned or have a transcript in Word format that made is available simultaneously with the video (on the same date that the video is made available or assigned to be watched).
- All content is accessible via the computer's keyboard, without the use of a mouse.

During the 2013–14 academic year, the first courses were reviewed. To successfully pass the review, each course had to meet twenty-six essential standards and 80 percent of the overall standards. The instructional designers worked closely with the Office of Distributed Learning, University Libraries, SDRC, and faculty to revise online courses.

The reviews were conducted by CTE instructional designers and were approved by the provost's DL committee. Faculty had access to the CTE instructional designers and were eligible to receive a small course revision grant. In addition to the grant, faculty received a commendation letter from the vice provost who is in charge of DL. The commendation letter was also sent to the faculty member's department chair and dean. Course reviews started on graduate programs (School of Library and Information Science, Nursing, and Communication Sciences and Disorders) during the following year.

CTE and Campus Partner Collaborations

Instructional designers facilitate an Instructional Designer Community of Practice (IDCoP) at the CTE. The IDCoP provides a space where staff brainstorm ideas, provide updates, share resources, and showcase examples of online learning best practices. Individuals who are involved in the IDCoP include instructional designers, directors or managers of online learning within the USC system, librarians, technology support personnel, and online learning professionals from across the state of South Carolina.

The CTE develops a calendar of events each fall and spring semester. Programming includes diversity and inclusive teaching workshops. Individuals from the CTE and campus partners conduct workshops on course accessibility, UDL, assistive technologies, approaches to fostering inclusion in the classroom, and more. Campus partners include individuals from the SDRC, Division of Information Technology, Office of Diversity and Inclusion, School of Library and Information Science, and the USC School of Medicine—Rehabilitation Counseling Program. CTE instructional designers and SDRC staff are invited by various units on campus to discuss accessibility in departmental meetings.

The CTE offers an eight-week short course, "Getting Started Teaching Online at USC," each fall and spring semester. This fully online course is offered with support from the Office of the Provost and has the goal of supporting and developing a community of faculty prepared to develop and teach high-quality online courses. Any faculty member who teaches as instructor of record at USC–Columbia or the Palmetto College campuses may apply, including adjunct faculty. Enrollees who successfully complete the course receive a small grant, a certificate of completion, and a letter of commendation from the CTE director. A week of the course is devoted to accessibility and UDL. Many faculty didn't consider accessibility before the short course and expressed an appreciation for the accessibility course materials.

The CTE also offers a short course "Teaching Online for Graduate Students." The eight-week course introduces graduate students to online teaching and develops their knowledge and ability for implementing and teaching online courses at USC and throughout their career. The goal of the course is to support and develop a community of graduate students prepared to develop and teach high-quality online courses. A week is devoted to accessibility and UDL.

The CTE established a Distributed Learning Summit. Key individuals involved in online learning on campus meet to discuss updates and challenges, seek assistance, and work together on various assignments each month. Involved offices include the CTE, Office of Distributed Learning, University Libraries, On Your Time Initiatives, Division of Information Technology, Palmetto College, and the SDRC. Campus partners discuss ways to remove barriers for students with and without disabilities.

The Office of Distributed Learning has two recording studios for faculty. These studios include instructional technologies that are used in an online environment. Dragon Naturally Speaking, a speech-to-text program, is also loaded on the computers. Staff at the Office of Distributed Learning help faculty create transcripts for lecture videos and audio presentations. The College of Nursing at USC–Columbia purchased Dragon Naturally Speaking for faculty to help with creating accessible lectures. The School of Library and Information Science conducts its own accessibility trainings for faculty.

Before a class can be converted from face-to-face to an online course, a faculty senate instructional development committee reviews course syllabi for quality. The committee uses a rubric to check for a wide variety of components, some of which include the following:

- course designator, number, and title
- academic bulletin description
- measurable learning outcomes
- overview of how the course will be conducted
- specific technologies to be used in the course
- minimum technical requirements and skills
- rubric information
- grading policy
- statement that identifies provisions and resources for students with disabilities
- statement with the university's academic integrity policy
- module-by-module schedule for course topics and activities
- justification for offering the course online

The committee consists of faculty, representatives from the CTE and University Libraries, student representatives, and other key university stakeholders.

School of Library and Information Science Quality Reviewed Courses

The School of Library and Information Science (SLIS) at USC expressed interest in becoming one of the first graduate programs to be quality reviewed. Representatives from the Office of Distributed Learning and the CTE met with SLIS faculty and support staff to discuss the process. To date, twelve SLIS courses have passed the quality review.

SLIS wanted to proactively create accessible online courses. Two faculty created professional development workshops for faculty and staff on how to create accessible Word documents, PowerPoint presentations, PDF files, and instructional videos.

New Distributed Learning Quality Review Process

Beginning in 2018, the DLQR process changed to provide increased collaboration among units on campus. Part of the new process is to develop a peer reviewer program consisting of faculty who will conduct reviews both within and external to their college or school. Instructional designers from the CTE will continue to conduct reviews and will be partnering with faculty peer reviewers to review courses. The CTE recruits potential faculty peer reviewers from each college and school and provides faculty funds to complete the Quality Matters program "Applying the Quality Matters Rubric" and "Peer Reviewer Course." A training module will be created to introduce the faculty peer reviewers to the process. Reviewers will serve a two-year term and receive stipends. The faculty will be recognized for their service and will be showcased on the CTE's website. In addition to serving as faculty peer reviewers, the faculty will serve as champions for quality online courses in their colleges and departments and around the university.

Conclusion

The CTE at the University of South Carolina–Columbia continues to seek partnerships on campus to cultivate diverse learning environments for students. Collaborating with administration, librarians, faculty, and other staff plays a vital role in creating a culture on campus of proactively creating accessible and universally designed online courses. Ideas in this chapter have worked for our faculty and students and are easy to integrate into any instruction. Hopefully this chapter has given you some ideas to pursue in your own learning institution. By working to create a culture of accessibility and universal design, your institution can more readily reach your mission of being more accessible to all users.

Notes

1. Elaine Allen and Jeff Seaman, *Grade Change: Tracking Online Education in the United States* (Oakland, CA: Babson Survey Research Group and Quahog Research Group, January 2014), http://sloanconsortium.org/publications/survey/grade-change-2013.
2. Amy Catalano, "Improving Distance Education for Students with Special Needs: A Qualitative Study of Students' Experiences with an Online Library Research Course," *Journal of Library and Information Services in Distance Learning* 8, no. 1/2 (2014): 17–31, https://eric.ed.gov/?id=EJ1032235.
3. Thomas J. Tobin, "Universal Design in Online Courses: Beyond Disabilities," *Online Cl@ssroom* 13, no. 12 (December 2013): 1–3, http://www.engl.duq.edu/servus/cv/Online.Classroom.13.12.pdf.
4. Catalano, "Improving Distance Education."
5. Tobin, "Universal Design in Online Courses."
6. About page, University of South Carolina, accessed March 8, 2018, http://www.sc.edu/about/.
7. Quality Matters homepage, MarylandOnline, accessed March 8, 2018, http://qualitymatters.org.
8. Heather Moorefield-Lang, Clayton Copeland, and Aisha Haynes, "Accessing Abilities: Creating Innovative Accessible Online Learning Environments and Putting Quality into Practice," *Education for Information* 32, no. 1 (2016): 27–33.

Chapter 8

Access through Universal Design and Technology

Stacy Hammer*

My first goal as a school librarian is to provide access for my patrons. By providing access to books, online reference materials, and tools through our makerspace, I give students opportunities for learning in many different ways through library programming. The availability of these materials alone meets the needs of some learners, but not all. What of the learners who need additional support? The reluctant learners? The learners who struggle with reading? The learners who are learning English while at school and speak another language at home? Additional support is needed by some learners in the library to make access for all possible.

By incorporating technology into lessons, students at a variety of ability levels can learn and show what they have been taught. The use of pictures, video, and audio, thanks to technology, can bring learning alive to students who do not learn well from traditional lecture and text reading. Beyond that, the inclusion of such technology opportunities is motivating for all learners and encourages creativity, collaboration, and digital competence. The library is not a place just for high-level readers, but a space where all learners of all abilities can find common ground.

The elementary school library where I work has approximately 650 students. It is nestled in a community halfway between our nation's capital and the Virginia state capital, Richmond. In this public school, there are a variety of learning needs, including but not limited to students who speak English as a second language, students with individualized education plans, and students with special needs. All students in the school attend a forty-five-minute library class once a week. Through this library class, students receive instruction in accordance with a library curriculum, which includes, but is not limited to, literature, research, digital citizenship, using library resources, makerspace, and coding. Students also use this forty-five-minute block of time to choose and check out library books. I want to create opportunities for meaningful instruction that will help my students grow as learners once they leave library class. I have found the best way to access all learners is by incorporating opportunities to learn and show learning through technology platforms.

Using technology in this way draws upon the theory of universal design. Universal design is planning spaces or products in a way that they are functional for as many people as possible.[1] The concept draws upon the design of making spaces usable for all, without marginalizing any group. For instance, wheelchair ramps at the mall are helpful for those in a wheelchair, but they are also useful to families pushing strollers and people who would rather walk the ramp than the stairs. In terms of libraries, it's making the physical space and programming accessible to all learners no matter their learning style, level, or ability. In terms of teaching and learning, having the opportunity to show learning via a platform that is heavy in pictures, videos, and audio does not take any learning away from the learners who can read and write at or above grade level. It does

* **Stacy Hammer** is a second-year elementary school librarian at Battlefield Elementary School in Spotsylvania, Virginia. A Michigan native, she is a graduate of Wayne State University and the University of Michigan. Before earning a School Librarianship Endorsement from Longwood University, she taught middle school English. She loves children's books, kayaking, her two dogs, and Vernors ginger ale. She lives in Fredericksburg, Virginia, with her husband and their two children.

bring the lesson or assessment to a place where all learners can succeed.

Universal Design for Learning (UDL) comes from Anne Meyer, David H. Rose, and David Gordon, authors of the book *Universal Design for Learning.* The framework they developed has three guiding principles—engagement, representation, and action and expression.[2] Incorporating lessons that can engage learners on many levels, represent content in many ways, and allow choice for students to demonstrate their learning using tools that align with their learning needs and styles in technology lessons increases the level of learning for all library patrons and promotes a more inclusive setting that has more flexibility for all users.[3]

Visual

In the context of teaching and learning, the concept of UDL begins during instruction. Our library is equipped with an interactive panel television. Working through a computer, the flat panel screen allows opportunities for students to work interactively through lessons and collaboratively after lessons have ended. The use of images and videos on the screen is a motivation; the interactive option is extremely encouraging as students may move and manipulate words and images to show their learning. By using not just words, but words and pictures during interactive activities, more students are able to access the learning. Kindergarten students who do not speak English at home are thrilled to show their understanding of the events in a story by sorting the pictures of the story events in order. The ability to use images, or images and words, makes the interactive board a tool that is universally beneficial to all students.

The library also has an interactive table available for students and teachers. Just as the interactive panel television encourages all learners by allowing them to manipulate pictures and words, the interactive table works in the same way. The flat panel television is used for whole-group instruction, small-group instruction, and small-group practice. The interactive table is perfect for small-group instruction and small-group practice. Again, the use of pictures and words in any manipulation makes the use of this design meaningful to more students. As students use pictures that are labeled with words in an interactive way, they are also building upon language skills and becoming stronger readers.

By using the platform of Google for Education, or GApps, students may complete formative and summative assignments by using little to no written text. This does not mean those who can write well do not get the opportunity to write; rather, it provides students more options to choose a format to meet their strengths.

Using Google Slides as an option for students to show their learning is as fantastic as it is versatile. By inserting a variety of pictures, students may answer a question or provide other evidence of learning. Students may search for pictures via a Google search, or they may take pictures themselves using the computer's camera function. Students can also create pictures themselves using Google's Draw function. By offering a variety of options and choices between images and words, students are able to select a combination that best meets their needs. An example of using Google Slides in the library plays upon the popular "selfie." Most students know what a selfie is, and many librarians have heard of a "shelfie," in which a person poses with a book. Fifth graders were assigned a slide number on a shared Google Slide, which had a book title on each slide. Students practiced their skills at using our online catalog. They found the book on the shelf using the call number and then took a "shelfie" of themselves with the book using the camera function on the Chromebook, which inserted the picture on the slide. After modeling, all fifth graders were able to navigate Google Slides and were able to show their ability to find a book using our online catalog. On the assessment end, it was a quick way to visually see which students can complete the task and which students need more instruction and practice with the skill.

Flipgrid is an online platform that educators can use to provide students an opportunity to show their answers through video. Teachers and librarians pose questions on Flipgrid and provide the link to students, and then their students record a short video. It is incredibly easy to use and encourages students to show their learning verbally, rather than through writing. This is a great way to encourage students to be creative in the way they film and to accommodate their needs as learners and sharers. Flipgrid is an excellent technology option to meet all learners where they are. On the assessment side, teachers may watch each video, leave comments, and use the grading rubric included on the video if they want to.

Audio

To make online text available to all students, our school district has acquired a program to read text aloud—Snap and Read. The program, used via a Chrome extension, can be opened by students, and it will remain open along the side of the window. When students do not know how to pronounce a word or would like to hear the text, they may highlight the desired text, and the program will read it aloud. This can be any text, anywhere. It will read websites, e-books, presentations, and documents. Once students are taught how to use the Chrome extension, using the read-aloud function is user-friendly. English language learners or anyone with an interest in other languages can change the settings in the program, so English text can be read aloud in a variety of languages. Spanish, French, Arabic, and more are available. Beyond the read-aloud function, Snap and Read also has a platform to write notes and outlines during researching and has capabilities to create citations. As a tool to universally assist teachers and students in teaching and learning, Snap and Read is designed in a way that all students can benefit from some of the tools, and those who benefit by hearing the text can listen to anything that is in electronic form.

For some students, the act of typing is difficult or downright impossible. To meet the needs of students who struggle with typing or physically cannot type, the use of the Google Voice typing tool is an option. As our library is equipped with a class set of Chromebooks, all students may submit work electronically. By using the Voice typing tool, students may speak the words they want written and watch them appear on the document. By using this tool, students of various ages and abilities can submit typed assignments to show their learning. Their work all looks the same, and some of the issues of spelling, grammar, and illegible handwriting are taken out of the assessment equation.

Interactive Books

Some resources seem to cross the line between a visual tool and an audio tool and between a teaching tool and a learning tool. The Lightbox by Follett is one such resource. Part e-book, part interactive learning center, the Lightbox combines reading with a read-aloud option, pictures, videos, maps, and links to outside websites on topics. Each book must be purchased via Follett, and the interactive book is available with unlimited copies for users, meaning all students in a class could have the e-book open at the same time. In the library, this resource can be used for research and more. When a librarian is collaborating with a classroom teacher, this resource is an option for the whole group, a small group, or individual instruction. As it can be read, listened to, and watched, it meets learners' strengths in a variety of ways. When paired with a tool like Snap and Read, it also becomes more accessible to more students, including English language learners.

Conclusion

With the variety of resources that are available for students, teachers, and librarians, some may say we are lucky. However, these resources are meaningless if students cannot access them or gain learning through them. Student access is the driving force that I consider often when planning lessons and reflecting on benefit and accessibility after lessons. As a librarian, it is easy for me to focus on physical accessibility. Can the students find and get the books they need? Is the makerspace set up in a way that all students have opportunities? Is there a way to change the layout to make more students want to enter our space? The list of questions to ponder is endless, and these all come back to universal design as well. As librarians we should consider taking the concept of universal design a step further into Universal Design for Learning—to not only make technology physically available for students, but also teach students how to use tools that will make the technology meaningful for teaching and learning as well.

Notes

1. "What Is Universal Design: Definition and Overview," Centre for Excellence in Universal Design, National Disability Authority, Dublin, Ireland, 2012, http://universaldesign.ie/What-is-Universal-Design/Definition-and-Overview/.
2. Anne Meyer, David H. Rose, and David Gordon, *Universal Design for Learning: Theory and Practice* (Wakefield, MA: CAST, 2014).
3. Carli Spina, "How Universal Design Will Make Your Library More Inclusive," *School Library Journal* 63, no. 5 (May 2017), https://www.slj.com/2017/05/diversity/how-universal-design-will-make-your-library-more-inclusive/#_.

Notes

Library Technology REPORTS

Upcoming Issues	
July 54:5	**Integrating the Library in the Learning Management System** edited by Amanda Clossen
August/ September 54:6	**Virtual and Augmented Reality** by Hannah Pope